Praise for the author

The words tenacious, caring and loving certainly apply to Sandi Allan, who is among many other things a gifted writer, painter and a true humanitarian in every sense of the word.

She has fought for and believes passionately in women's rights and can speak first hand on many aspects of the subject, which she does so eloquently in this book. I have known and worked alongside Sandi for many decades. She is a loyal and long standing friend to many, myself included and I have always been impressed with her work ethic and her generosity of spirit toward her fellow citizens.

Ron Johanson OAM ACS
Roly Poly Picture Company Qld Australia.

I first met Sandi Allan in the mid eighties when she worked as a production and location manager in the Australian film industry. I have followed her journey closely through the ten difficult years in Bali and her eventual safe return to Australia, culminating in the writing of this book.

I believe this book to be a fine testimony to Sandi's courage, resilience and will to find meaning and purpose in extremely difficult and sometimes dangerous circumstances.

Kurt Olsen
Short Film Maker, Writer & Portrait Artist

I am proud to call Sandi my friend and can vouch for her honesty and caring for others.

If I ever need help of any sort I would certainly ask her knowing she would be there.

Kawena Gordon
Author and Professional Public Speaker.

Sandi you write so beautifully. You have a very generous heart and spirit which comes through so clearly in your compelling story which I am sure will help many women. I am truly privileged to have been part of the process of your book. I think you have done an excellent job and wish you every success in the future.

Louise (surname withheld)
Editor

Some Local Inside Information

I wish to dedicate these pages to sharing some advice and hope you may receive it as a bit of local inside information to assist, guide and protect those who plan to move to Bali, Indonesia or to any other 3rd world country or countries with cultural differences from Western society. I was a naïve, vulnerable woman travelling on my own who believed and trusted everyone. Through my experience I hope and pray that I will be able to save other women from experiencing what I have gone through. Local women have also succumbed to a similar fate but sadly there is little they can do about it, mainly because of fear and intimidation. While there are many successful expats living in Bali, there are hundreds of stories never told; not only by women but men also. You hear the stories all the time as you get to know people.

It is so easy to be swept up in the moment and a woman on her own is a target. It does not matter what your age is, what your shape is or how you look. Don't do as I did. I now realise that before embarking on such a journey and to move to an unfamiliar country it's important to look beyond the glitz, glamour and with respect, sales pitch and discounts of even the most helpful travel agent. I did not go there for the high life and glitz and I surely did not go there expecting to face the experiences that I had.

Investigate, in detail, the country you are going to reside in especially where it is strongly represented by their beliefs, day to day living, culture and religions. Whether you are religious or not, it is very helpful to understand the basics, at the very least. There is a very good government organisation with English speaking officials in Bali, dealing with human rights for women and who can assist you in matters of domestic abuse and violence.

If you move there, try to learn the language as soon as possible. There are courses you can take. Put yourself first and this way you won't fall into the pits. People will help you but you need to be aware that it usually comes at a price. Until you physically live in an environment, no matter how much you see on a television screen or what is in the brochures, none of it will prepare you for what is ahead.

Remain alert whether you are enjoying a holiday or residing in Bali. Trust your instincts and observe what is happening around you. If you sense that something does not feel right ask around or find some western business people who live there to chat to. If things are spiraling out of control for you seek help as soon as you can. There is now a Bali business directory you can get which has valuable information and there is a western paper called The Bali Advertiser which is free in supermarkets.

Take note of government rulings. The laws change constantly and one must read between the lines and keep up to date with the changes as much as possible. Be aware that you can go and seek advice from six different people and often you will walk away with six different interpretations of the one thing.

Understand that there are thousands of different dialects of the Indonesian language. The common use of the Indonesian Bashan language is very different from the literal translation of words and sentences and their meanings. The main ones you will come across in Bali, for example, are; Balinese Indonesian, straight Indonesian if I can describe it that way, Javanese and the Lombok dialect but then you will come across Sumatran, Sulawesi, Kupang or the languages of East Timor, now known as Timor Leste, Surabaya, Jakarta and many others.

Know the currency and remember that it is always much better to change your money at a well sign posted authorised money changer once you have left the airport.

Be respectful of dress codes e.g. a male or female expat sitting in a restaurant with very little clothing on (men not wearing shirts) is frowned upon by local people.

If you happen to get into a fight (men), do not hit a local. You will find yourself in big trouble even if you were hit first. These types of

situations are frequent in many night clubs and the more popular bars and hotel club scenes.

Protect your belongings wherever you go; your phone, bag, wallet and any valuables. Lock your doors at night even when staying in a secure compound, villa or resort. You should also lock your bathroom doors. Especially protect your bag and jewelry on a motorbike. I have witnessed and personally rescued local women on busy highways being sideswiped by other motorbikes and robbed. They have been left badly injured on the highway while their motorbike catapults down the road with sparks flying.

If you have children with you and you decide to get a massage anywhere, do not leave your children alone or with staff. There are a lot of perpetrators everywhere who come across as helpful and friendly. You don't want your children having their innocence ripped away from them. This does happen.

Don't accept drinks from anyone, especially in night clubs, and don't leave your drink on the bar and go off dancing.

If you are going to ride or be a pillion passenger on a motorbike you must wear a helmet and clothing for protection. If you have ever assisted someone who has fallen from a motorbike you will know what I am talking about. The burns and scaring you are left with are ugly and if you have the misfortune to have worse injuries but don't have insurance you have a huge problem. No hospital will attend you until it has been cleared with your insurance company that they will pay. This is a huge problem in Bali and there are many complaints written to the papers.

Never drink the local water unless you want Bali belly or other stomach viruses. Trust me, it will ruin your holiday or hinder your settlement into your new lifestyle.

Nowadays there are some very good hospitals and pharmacies for medication and treatment as well as some very good international schools for children. Be aware that many of the more mature local men and woman have no schooling. They are a very creative nation and will amaze you with what they can create from nothing, but they do not have the same reasoning or logic as we do. This can often cause confusion, confrontation and a loss in patience. Generally, they are a gentle race but have many methods that we do not apply in situations when dealing with people, animals or the running of a home and business.

It is polite to take your shoes off when entering someone's home, no matter what form that is. It is impolite to touch people on the head even in a kind display however, the younger generation is becoming more westernised.

You will find local women of Indonesia do not wear swim suits to go in a pool or swim in the ocean, they are always covered however, you will find that the men strip down to bathers or just their underpants. You may 'not' go topless at any beach or resort in Indonesia; this is a huge no-no.

Make sure your visa is the right one and keep up-to-date with changes in regulation and the law. Find a reliable source to get the best advice, then double-check it. If you marry an Indonesian, from any of the islands, you cannot leave Indonesia without the written approval of the spouse which is submitted to the government and immigration; they decide whether you can go offshore or overseas or not and stipulate for how long you may go. You are then issued an exit-reentry permit, which you pay for.

When you live in Indonesia, whether short or long term, you must have a police permit which is to be renewed each time your visa is renewed. Failure to do this can result in huge fines and/or a term of imprisonment.

Sympathetic tolerance from expats living in Bali is wearing thin towards those who get caught with or using drugs, as you will often read in the local papers. Yes, there are drugs everywhere in Bali and yes, it is very easy for those who participate in the taking of them to acquire some. You can, and at some stage most probably will, be approached while walking along the streets of Kuta and other areas but be warned, often this is a trap and don't think for a moment that you are invincible. Parents, if you value your son or daughter's life and they are visiting

Bali, please strongly warn them they can find themselves being arrested before they can even blink their eyes. You can be set up very easily and there is undetectable intelligence everywhere, day and night.

It is extremely inadvisable to drink the local 'arak' alcohol in small cafés or local warung food places anywhere in Bali. Often these are illegal mixes with literally deadly consequences as arak is mixed with lethal, life threatening toxins. Many people of varying ages and from many countries have died after consuming this drink. Reports are often in the local western paper of the latest deaths. There is nothing doctors can do to save a victim; death comes painfully quickly. Police do their best to find and destroy the sources and outlets but it is an uphill battle as it is produced in the back alleys.

It is essential to find out if your own country has some sort of alliance with another country but this does not mean you have a safety net or assistance at your fingertips if or when you need it. Your consulate in another country does not help in private or personal matters, no matter what the situation is. It doesn't matter which 3rd world country you go to, you will meet most, if not all, the same sorts of circumstances and dangers e.g. the Philippines, Africa, India, South America and Mexico. Be aware at all times and don't make hasty decisions when swept up in the exotic atmosphere.

Never be in a hurry to agree to anything, even if you feel overtaken with emotion and empathy.

If you are feeling undecided about a situation in any way, it is wise not to be intimidated by someone's words or advice, the quick approach or excuses being given or actions taken when trying to persuade you in a certain direction. This usually means there is more going on than you are being led to believe. Body language, eyes, talk and laughter do not match up! And if there is more than one person involved usually one plays off against the other using gestures, some very subtle and quick while others are over the top.

2. Indonesia is known as the ring of fire and some places burn hotter than others.

BROKEN
Dolls of Bali

Global Publishing Group
Australia • New Zealand • Singapore • America • London

BROKEN Dolls of Bali

A True Story Of Broken Dreams;
What's Not In The Travel Brochures That Every
Woman Should Know.

Sandi Allan

DISCLAIMER

All the information, techniques, skills and concepts contained within this publication are of the nature of general comment only and are not in any way recommended as individual advice. The intent is to offer a variety of information to provide a wider range of choices now and in the future, recognising that we all have widely diverse circumstances and viewpoints. Should any reader choose to make use of the information contained herein, this is their decision, and the contributors (and their companies), authors and publishers do not assume any responsibilities whatsoever under any condition or circumstances. It is recommended that the reader obtain their own independent advice.

First Edition 2014

Note, some names have been changed in this book for protection and privacy.

National Library of Australia
Cataloguing-in-Publication entry:

Allan, Sandi, author.

Broken dolls of Bali : a true story of broken dreams : what's
not in the travel brochures that every woman should know / Sandi Allan.

1st ed.
ISBN: 9781922118318 (paperback)

Women travelers--Handbooks, manuals, etc

Intercultural communication--Indonesia--Bali
(Province)--Handbooks, manuals, etc.
International travel--Indonesia--Bali (Province)
Bali (Indonesia : Province)--Social life and customs--Handbooks, manuals, etc

910.202

Published by Global Publishing Group
PO Box 517 Mt Evelyn, Victoria 3796 Australia
Email info@TheGlobalPublishingGroup.com

For Further information about orders:
Phone: +61 3 9736 1156 or Fax +61 3 8648 6871

I Dedicate my book to all Abused or Violated Women and Children around the World.
Let us unite as one voice to stop all violence, abuse, rape and atrocities. Speak out against violence; silence only gives permission for perpetrators to continue their abuse.

Sandi Allan

Acknowledgements

I have been incredibly humbled by the love and unconditional support that I received while going through my hellish journey and the extreme lessons it has taught me.

Firstly, to the most wonderful daughters and son I have been blessed with; I thank you from the deepest part of my heart and soul. Your love and support kept me alive when I was tempted to allow my mind to go to the dark place of giving up.

My darling children, Angila and Phil Pluis, thank you so very much for everything, for your love and your support in everything you did for me and the sacrifices you made. I know it was not fun for you, worrying whether I would make it out alive and I am sorry you had to bear my problems.

Nartasha Alger, thank you for your love and support during these past years. I know it was very difficult for you. You also sacrificed a lot for me, even giving up your well deserved annual leave to come and see if I was safe. Your help in so many ways kept me going and your words of encouragement resonated in my ears in so many difficult times. I am sorry for all the worry I caused you.

Shane Davies, thank you my son for your love and support and your loving words. I felt your hugs from across the ocean.

Thank you so much to my family back in my birth country, Thank you for your love and tremendous support in every way possible. I will never forget.

To my wonderful neighbour, Jane Runtuwene, you are a treasure. Your generosity and the unconditional support you have shown me since becoming aware of my situation have been undeniably amazing. I thank you so much for your love and not only for being my confidante but without a doubt you definitely were my lifeline. You surely were God's gift to me. May the Lord watch over you always and bless you in all things. Thank you also to Joyce Schindler for your love and beautiful friendship and thank you to Najwa Green for everything entrusted to me by you and your warm friendship.

I wish to thank Henk de Nes (APEX Expertise) for all your superb help, assistance and friendship.

Thank you also to my other wonderful friends, H & N.J. who sheltered and protected me, supported me in many ways and were my friends. I will always remember and be forever grateful. Thank you to Dianna for your great help.

Thank you so much Arini and Gustu and Wira for all your help and support which was always unconditional and so generous and kind. May God always watch over you and bless you. Thank you to Lu Putu for hanging in there and fighting the long and hard battle with me till the end.

Guy Joseph, thank you for helping and assisting me when I needed help, a friend who brightened my day and gave me hope. I wish you success with the orphanage and all your programs to assist the disadvantaged people in the coming years.

To my dear sweet friend, Novina Dominica (Nona), thank you for your beautiful friendship. You are an angel; giving of yourself to me and everyone in your life so unselfishly. I will miss your soulful singing and your warm spirit but know you will always be in my heart dear friend. May God watch over you and bless you with love in return for all those you help and have helped in your life.

To Ron Johanson OAM ACS, a dear friend with a huge heart; thank you so much Ron for all your wonderful support, encouragement and beautiful energy. You have always been there for me, thank you so much for holding out your hand to me. As you always say to me, God love ya Ronny.

To my friend, Kurt Olsen, you have been my rock. Many thanks mate, for just being you. Your honesty, concern and caring over the years has been with total unconditional generosity. Nobody could wish for a more wonderful friend to have in their life. I feel honoured and blessed to be your friend.

Thank you to Alex and Mike you are true treasures.

My lifelong friend of forty years, Angela Kraushaar, thank you my darling friend; we have been through thick and thin together and no matter what the distance, near or far, you have always been there. You are an amazing lady and I am privileged to be dear friends with you. Your spirit and integrity uplift me whenever we share time together.

To my darling girlfriend Jillian Rollo, Jewels you have been my precious angel and I so thank you for all your love, help and support. During my worst times I would see your face and your crystal clear sparkling eyes in my mind and they would always lift me. You are a treasured soul who will always have a special place in my heart.

To Di McLaren and Russ Duparcq, thank you so very much for all your love, support, kind thoughts and help. I will hold you very dear to me always.

My lovely angel friend, Nili Ben-David, thank you so much for your hope, inspiration and friendship. I will always hold you dear in my heart for your love and generosity of unconditional support. Bless you. I wish to sincerely thank my proof reader Louise for the outstanding commitment to me and my book. Her dedication has been truly amazing and her personal reflection of my book to me.

I wish to thank my friends Ikhlas and Yanni Syuriansah for all your support and friendship. Rian and Guru, thank you for your endless efforts to keep me in touch with my family and friends. I will always remember.

To my lovely spiritual friend, Mary Naraya, thank you so very much for all your mail, love and support. Your guidance and words of wisdom kept me grounded. Bless you always.

To Sharon (Wolf) Spirit Whisperer, thank you sweet lady for all we shared. Your support I will always remember. You are a beautiful spirit and soul. Your selfless devotion to helping others though risking your own life, enduring much bodily and emotional pain many times, is to be honored.

To Col Noble, Australian entertainer and singer, thank you for your kind support, friendship and advice.

A huge thank you to Darren Stephens and Jackie Stephens, your inspiration, belief in me and your guidance has been nothing short of brilliant. Thank you for your incredible mentoring. I could not have done this without you and the Global Publishing team.

Thank you to Les & Mitch, Pomona News Agency, Sunshine Coast, Queensland, for your generous support, inspiration and trust.

Special thanks to Gay Warner, 'A Touch of The Past' coffee shop, Pomona, Sunshine Coast, Queensland, for sharing your dolls.

Thank you also to Vicki Hull. Noosaville, Queensland, for your encouragement, enthusiasm and great wisdom and guidance.

Thank you to all the friends who sent love and messages through my family to me. It meant so much to me. I will always be grateful. Bless you all always.

There are no words powerful enough that can say what I feel in my heart for the pure love, support and attention I have received since 2010. I will forever be eternally grateful to everyone. Thank you so much.

Sandi Allan

Contents

Chapter One

The Inexperienced Traveller

Chapter One
The Inexperienced Traveller

A couple of times I found myself gazing in the local travel agents windows when going to do some usual home supply shopping. I would ponder on the thoughts in my mind as my heady friend had a debate with me, you should go, no I can't, yes you can, but what if, and so on until the next time I found myself standing before racks of books and brochures in the travel agents office. I felt overwhelmed by the hundreds of places on offer around the globe. My mind was blank.

I heard a voice over my shoulder saying, "Can I help you, is there somewhere in particular you want to go?" I turned to face the speaker and said, "I haven't a clue really, I know I need to go somewhere peaceful, with culture and somewhat spiritual."

I took a seat at her desk and we discussed my thoughts on a destination. As I had been studying Native American Indians and Shamanism healings and rituals I said I would like to spend some time at a Native American reservation and learn more. She knew of someone who had done this previously and suggested that I would probably be disappointed as the reservations were not so traditional any more. That was a blow to me and I said that I didn't know where else to go then to which she replied that Bali, Indonesia has culture and being known as the Island of the Gods it would be a spiritual environment to consider. I knew nothing about Bali or Indonesia only what I had heard from a few people who'd been there several years before. So off I went home with a handful of brochures to look over on the different areas which included other islands besides Bali.

I returned a few days later and said okay, I would go there. We worked out my itinerary for different places to visit and stay. I decided that I would take my time and have a good look around while I was there. She got back to me with my flight and accommodation bookings which included going to two other islands besides covering Bali from one side

to the other. I purchased a Lonely Planet book to read up on traditions, what to do and not to do, dress and acceptable attire in the areas I was going to and the usual points of interest.

My travel agent treated me with the gift of being picked up, by a limo of all things.

So come departure day, my gate bell rings just after dawn and I go out to find this enormous white stretch limo sitting in my driveway. I could not believe it and burst out laughing. "You have got to be joking," I said to my driver. "Yes, my dear," he said, "all for you." Wow....I was stunned. I got in and off we went down my farm road.

We got into my local town area and he seemed to be turning the wrong way at the roundabout but he said it was just a short diversion. I wondered what it was and he said, "Just look out your window as we come around the roundabout." Lo and behold, there standing on the sidewalk at the crack of dawn was my lovely travel agent, Sharon. She was giving me the Queens wave. I broke into laughter as I returned a badly impersonated Queens wave to her. It was hilarious but I felt so blessed by this lovely lady and the trip she had prepared for me.

On arrival at the international terminal I felt really shy getting out of this amazing vehicle. What a ride I had experienced. People were gazing at me as I got out. My driver said, "I will see you in a few weeks when I will be here to pick you up on your return home." It felt like eyes were on me on board my flight, wondering who this woman was. Ha, they would have been disappointed to learn I was nobody in particular.

On my arrival I had no idea what to expect so just followed the crowd heading down long corridors, which seemed endless. I went through customs which was fine and uneventful. I had been warned not to take help from some guy who wanted to help with my luggage and thought I was onto it but then someone with a badge on came up to me and I thought it was helpful airport staff....

Helpful yes, airport staff not! He was one of the many guys trying to earn a buck or two as I found out when I got outside to meet my organised private driver and guide. This guy was yelling at me saying pay…pay….pay but he didn't understand what I was saying so my guide informed me that I must pay him for taking my bags, however, now there were two of them with their hands out to me. I had not changed any of my money so instantly I panicked as I was not used to having someone aggressively asking me for money. I dipped my hand into my wallet and handed him $5 and said that is all I have. I learned later that he would have been very happy because in 2003 it was far beyond any price they got for carrying a bag or two.

I was already freaking out and wondering what the hell I was doing in this place as I was driven to my first accommodation. My guide and driver both spoke some English, thank goodness.

The first resort was very nice however, I was too afraid to go outside onto the streets without going in the car. I ate at the internal restaurant and then after a few days they told me that there was also a restaurant at the end of the drive and which had music. I thought this would be better than sitting alone with no entertainment at the internal restaurant. I got ready that night to try the other but stood at the entrance looking way down towards the street, humming and harring for five minutes.

I had to really talk to myself and convince myself it was okay to go down there. In the end I was glad I had braved it as I could not believe my ears when I was listening to this singer from the band. I was eating outside and could only hear the music but could not see them play. After dinner I thought I would step inside and see who the person with this amazing voice was. I sat at the very back and just listened and enjoyed the evening.

I started getting harassed by the food and beverage manager. I would return to my bungalow and he would ring me and say, "Hello, I see you just returned to your bungalow, is there anything I can do for you?" "No

thank you," I'd reply. It happened again even at midnight and I thought he must be spying on me as there is no office near my bungalow. I very politely reported him to the reception and they said they would look into it. It happened again, so straight after his phone call I went to the reception and asked to speak to the manager. I had written a formal complaint out before going there. I asked reception to send a fax to my travel agent for me, which they did, and then I took it over to the manager and said I was laying a formal complaint. He apologised and actually told me they had had a lot of trouble with him before for doing this with other single women staying there. I wondered what the hell he was still doing there if they had had several complaints about him already.

Anyway, as I was booked back in there later on my trip I said to them that if they did not do something I would go elsewhere on my return and they could expect my agent to ask them to refund my, already paid, booking. So, for the next stay there they upgraded me to another area for safety.

My guide and driver would pick me up at around 9am each day and take me on the usual heavily populated and directed tourist spots that most everyone is taken to. Tanah Lot, Bedugul, Silver jewellers markets in Mas.

I was taken to Kintamani to view the sleeping volcano. A beautiful view but the harassment by the street vendors was so in your face that it not only terrified me but really aggravated me when they would not accept, 'No thank you, I don't want anything.' I could not wait to get out of there.

I travelled over to my first island which was quiet and relaxing with lots of brilliant massages by the resort's little masseur. On my return to Bali I felt very ill. I had picked up a rare stomach virus, not the usual Bali belly which is well known by travellers.

After learning from the Director (Australian Doctor) of the International Clinic I had, as he put it, the misfortune to get this bad stomach virus. I had a week of daily tests that had to be done. This was not only time consuming but with my itinerary was very difficult as I was quite some distance away and now staying in another area.

I had to cancel the 1 week course on Indonesian cooking classes I had booked and paid for, as I was not well enough to attend, so it was a big disappointment and there was no refund. My next accommodation was even further out, in fact on the other side of Bali, a good two or three hours drive depending on traffic and road conditions.

I lasted 24 hours at that one even though I had paid for seven nights. Still sick and seeing that I could not even get out of the gate onto the beach without coming face to face with beach merchants waiting right at the gate I decided I didn't want to be there. I had come away for peace, not to be harassed. I know they have to make a living and I don't mind buying things but this was just so in your face, constantly; it was too much for me.

I returned to Bali earlier than planned and went back to my first accommodation where they did keep their word on upgrading my booking for free and they also made sure the food and beverage manager did not contact me in any way.

I got to know the band a little better and one of the members could speak some English. I could not speak any Indonesian except for terima kasih (thank you), tidak (no), selamat pagi (good morning), selamat malam (good evening), tidak bli (I am not buying) and maaf (sorry). I bought the band some meals as they had told me they had been eating the same meal there for years, Nasi Goering, which the resort provided for them during their break. The singer said he wanted to talk to me but could not speak English. I said it was okay, so we did sign language, used items as examples and drew pictures. It was quite delightful. His beautiful, large brown eyes captivated me and his charisma, charm, soft voice

and infectiously gorgeous smile totally won me over. I was seduced by him in the moonlight, on a beach while the gentle waves lapped the shoreline. That's never happened before. Oh my! We got on really well. He said he wanted to learn English so I said I would help him while I was there. I took the band and their wives out for meals and outings. It was really nice. I felt safe with them and thought they would not do anything wrong as they could lose their jobs if something happened. After spending quite a bit of time with them they got to know that my work for 25 years, in Australia, was in the film and television industry. They asked me if I would become their manager so I said I would give it some thought and I did.

I said I would return and see how serious they were at getting themselves to a professional level as a group. There were a couple in the group that I was having those gut intuition signals on but generally it felt okay. Little did I realise that I had caught that other bug many get when they visit Bali. You have probably heard of or know someone who has caught it, it's the Bali seduction bug.

It is the one where the heat of the day makes you feel fantastic and those balmy moonlit nights with the gentle washing of waves that lick the shoreline give you a feeling of freedom; releasing all sense of rationale while other tantalising whispers seduce you.

I was bedazzled by the casual atmosphere surrounding local people. Even though they always seemed to be going somewhere or doing something they would just breeze through with a smile. The perfumed incense burning everywhere, night and day, the barong chime and beats in your ears seem to send you into a soft trance whether strolling through the streets or visiting markets filled with local people selling their wares. I had already picked up some of the local traditions by just observing quietly or asking a band member or his wife about different things. I was keen to learn and understand. For example, if you do get to eat with a local family you should only eat with your right hand and it is a good practice to fall into straight away, especially if it is a Muslim family or community. Take your shoes off before entering any of their

houses or dwellings whether they are Hindu or Muslim. Some Christian homes are more flexible. An easy rule of thumb is to follow what they do.

It shocked me however, to see such poverty as I was now being exposed to the real world of Bali, Indonesia not the highlife of nightclubs and boozing till dawn. It brought many tears to my eyes and being a person who wondered, as always, how I could help and what I could contribute, I did not realise that my vulnerability and naivety would become a target in the future. I have always trusted everyone at face value unless my intuition has given me other signals whereupon I would always keep my distance, not engaging myself past cordial greetings.

Before I left I had said to the band that I would come back later in the year and see how they were performing. I left a sum of money behind in a bank account for which I had calculated studio hire for five months so they could practice three times a week. I would also get reports from them once a week. I had taken professional photos of them, which I was going to get developed and enlarged back in Australia, to promote them at resorts etc. in Bali on my return.

I had learned all their family histories, much of which brought great sadness with overwhelming tears from me and immense empathy for them all. Everything seemed super fine at my departure, although it was emotional for me to leave the intoxicating shores of the Island of the Gods.

I felt a loss during my return flight back to Australia but gave thought to what I would need to do on returning to Bali in the future. My plan was to eventually do a tour of Australia with them, as my background had given me many good contacts and I had been an agent for actors and bands in my early days in the industry.

I settled back in on my property and found peace and joy with my animals and beautiful grounds. I set about doing research with the

government on what would be required, officially, to bring the band in for a tour and acquired all the necessary legal documents. I spoke with the union to make sure all the boxes would be ticked so there would be no difficulties or problems for them to work temporarily while in Australia. I had tapes that were recorded live as they performed at the resort and converted them to a CD for my return where I planned for them to do a professional CD recording of cover numbers for demo purposes and to promote them once they had reached a smooth professional level.

I had been asked to name the band so, while the photos were being processed and blown up to full poster size, I had T-shirts made with the band's name on them. During this process I came up with about ten names and emailed the list to the band so that they could choose one. They liked two in particular and after throwing it back and forth via email it was decided. I had four T-shirts made for each of them, so twenty in total, which I would take back with me on my return. I decided not to tell them I was doing this to give them extra incentive and encouragement along with the professional image when promoting them in Bali after I returned in October. I purchased two new acoustic guitars, a keyboard and a specialised indoor-outdoor performance microphone. They wanted some lyric song books which you just could not get in Indonesia, especially Bali, with the correct lyrics in English, so I went on a search to buy a good cross section of Blues, Ballads, Rock and Jazz music as this was the main style that they did best. The singer could sing anything and any style with a vocal range of five octaves; soft or powerful he could do it all.

Little did I know, when I returned to Bali, that I had made myself a great target for customs. I was still so naïve when travelling, especially going there with a stack of goodies. Sure enough, as soon as I hit the customs checking aisles, suddenly there was not one officer but a group of them questioning me! I said I was bringing my luggage and items in to help some of their people. I was marched away into the office where I had to explain to the chief of customs not only why I was bringing in so much stuff but how much it had cost me as I had to pay to bring it in. I had been told not to get into any discussions with customs officers

if questioned but I just couldn't help myself as I wasn't doing it for any profit, in fact it was quite the contrary. They assessed all my items and came up with a ridiculous penalty that I had to pay. I said I wouldn't pay that as I had come to help people, so didn't understand why I should be penalised for it. They eventually brought the penalty charges down a little but I knew I was going to have to cough up. I just wanted to get out of there as quickly as possible.

As I left the office still angry, I said to them, "Well, in future if I come back here I will bring nothing with me, you destroy all good intentions of empathy," and I left. Do you know that the next time I went to Bali they remembered my name and as I approached customs they were calling my name and saying hello? They have an incredible memory for recalling your name. I would open my bags and ask, "What do you want?" As their eyes glistened over my luggage, they would just hold me up while they continued to peruse everything without saying anything except, "What else do you have?" "Nothing, take what you want or let me go," would be my reply. My usual good manners had worn thin at the airport.

I was glad to meet up with the singer and lead guitarist of the band who had come to meet me, this time with the hired car which I had arranged before leaving Australia.

I checked into different accommodation than for my previous stay as I did not want to have the same problems with the food and beverage manager again. It was a quiet boutique resort in the same area of Sanur, which is thirty minutes or so from the noisy, fast-paced Kuta area.

I settled in and later the band gathered together to greeting me. I gave them their T-shirts which they were thrilled with, especially when they saw the band's name on them. In minutes the keyboard was up and running, which was music to my ears. They had some food and drink as a little celebration of my return during which we arranged to go out that evening to observe another venue, possibly at Nusa Dua. It was lovely

and one of the wives also came along.

After that it was down to work and studio practices so that I could hear firsthand how they were sounding. There had been problems with the drummer while I was in Australia so I had said they'd better find a replacement as I wasn't interested in him coming to Australia. I found out that he took drugs of some sort and was always asking to dip into the money I had sent for their band practice sessions. The other members were in constant contact with me while I was home in Australia so I knew fairly well what was going on most of the time. They had found another drummer more in their age group as this band was not of the younger set and just starting out, they all had at least twenty years experience as musicians in Bali and further afield.

They sounded much better than when I left. The new drummer had made a huge difference to the full sound of music they were playing. We had various meetings about this guy and whether he should or should not be in the band. I had my own concerns about him after learning that his wife was ill in hospital with cancer. This was a real worry as I had come with contracts drawn up for the band in another step to readiness not only as manager for them in Bali but also for the time when they would come to Australia. This is when a few of the true characteristics started to evolve. I had two members pushing for him to join as they were all in the same church together, (religion is a huge player in all things there) but one did not want him to join and was giving me reasons why not but could not express those thoughts openly in front of the group. It is one of the culturally unacceptable things over there. Two were fence sitters and would not say one way or the other. I started feeling uneasy as this new member wanted to have a meeting about joining the group but he was quite aggressive in his approach.

He held the floor in the meeting in which most of it was translated to me as he only knew a little English. I was taken aback by his demands, considering he was not yet officially in the group as far as I was concerned.

I also had to point out to him that I could not see how he would be able to travel to Australia with his wife so ill but he didn't seem to have a problem with that part. I handed out the contracts for them all to take away and read, as I had had them translated into Indonesian and also provided copies in English.

It was established that he was their preferred drummer overall, due to his experience, so it was agreed upon even though I had reservations.

Then, just before they were all due to leave, they dropped the bombshell on me that he needed to borrow some money from me as his wife couldn't leave the hospital until he had paid the bill. I said I didn't know if I could do that and asked how much he needed. I was shocked when they told me he wanted over a thousand dollars. I could feel myself panicking inside and also felt that I had been set up which angered me, but I could not show this. I said I would have to contact my accountant and would let them know. With that, it was suggested I should go with the singer to the hospital to see her for myself. It was arranged and we went late that afternoon. My intuition was giving me signals which made me more uncomfortable. The next day I was asked for a decision about him borrowing the money from me. I felt slightly intimidated by the eyes and ears that were paused to hear my reply.

With much reluctance I said that I would lend him the money on the condition that he sign a legal loan document and the legal quittance receipt of loan, making it totally legal. I gave him the money in front of the band and had them witness the transaction. I felt bad that I had these feelings of being trapped into giving the loan to him as his wife was terminally ill with cancer.

Within a day of lending him the money I learned just what a target I had become as another band member cried for money to pay his annual rent. He asked for $500 and was followed by another wanting $400 for his bike registration. Oh dear God, I thought, I cannot refuse them as this would cause big trouble. Once again, I entered a legal loan with them

as I had done with the drummer and all stated faithfully that they would pay back the loans. I had actually included in their contracts that if any member borrowed any money from me and they left the band for any reason, the loans had to be paid back in full if not already done. This had put a damper on my enthusiasm, so now I started treading more carefully with these guys.

The pleasant part of having been back for a few days was when the singer, Hass, said he wanted to talk to me about something. This had me intrigued as he suggested we go upstairs to where the keyboard was being kept in my villa accommodation. He got two pillows and put them on the floor and said, “Sit.” I thought this must be some tradition. He started to talk and I could not get a word in edgeways. I was blown away as he could hardly say a word in English when I left but he chattered on solidly for three hours and his English was fluent and I understood everything he was saying even though the grammar was a bit here and there. This gave me new hope and showed the effort he had put in. I felt all the phone calls and keeping his English going had really paid off. I even thought he had to have gone to classes, but he swore he hadn’t. It had been a lovely day after the negative outcome of the day before. We had a lovely meal which I cooked for us at the villa. He said this was the first time anyone had done this for him. I got a recipe from one of the wives and tried my uneducated Indonesian cooking on him. It had turned out quite well for a first attempt.

I felt the band was ready to make a recording so set up a day in the recording studio in Sanur. We were to record sixteen tracks live, all cover numbers, in one day. I prayed they would all turn up on time as we had no time to dilly dally around. Sure enough, when I arrived at the studio, everyone was waiting excitedly. I took my camera with me to get some good shots of them all recording and some casual buddy shots. It was a long day but we were done by six o’clock. I went back with a couple of the band members to mix and critique the tracks before the final mix. It all sounded great and we were so excited to go and listen in comfort to the recording. They were ecstatic, listening to themselves. It was celebration time for everyone.

My visit was coming to an end and I was due to depart again, when the keyboard player fell ill. I cancelled the flight I was booked on and moved my departure back by a week to take him to hospital and try to help. It really annoyed me when, during his examination in emergency at the hospital, he was told he seriously needed a blood transfusion and he said he wanted to go home. He refused further treatment so I just paid the bill and we took him back to his rented rooms.

A couple of nights later while sitting in my villa, I thought I should try to get some sleep as it was around 2am. This was not uncommon for me as I had not slept properly for a very long time. I lay down on the bed and thought it would be okay to get some shuteye but I suddenly woke up at about 5.30am when I needed to go to the loo. On the way, even though I was still in a sleepy state, I wondered where my new phone was. You see, I had just replaced my phone, which was only about two months old but during my stay it had been stolen. It was not a cheap phone and I had replaced it with another one just like it. I came back out of the bathroom and it hit me fair in the face.

My floor was covered with my belongings. I had been robbed while I lay sleeping for those few hours. Immediately I saw that my phone was gone as well as my new digital camera. I ran outside onto the verandah and could see more of my items spread across the lawn and the camera case that had my 35mm camera and lens in lay empty. I yelled that I had been robbed then went back into my room and rang for reception screaming that I had been robbed. I noticed the thieves had tried to get my laptop from beside me on the bedside table but thank God I had it securely locked and attached to the table with a strong cable. My bag was empty, my purse open and all the money that I had just got out of the reception safe to purchase things in the morning, was gone.

I rang Hass and told him, then remembered the keyboard in the upstairs room. My feet missed steps as I ran up to the second level. I let out a huge sigh as the door was still locked and after checking the room I saw the keyboard was still there. As I went up the steps I saw stuff scattered across neighbouring villas in the secured resort. There was clothing

everywhere and I knew it wasn't mine. The thieves had done six of us over in those early hours of the morning. What struck me the most was the fact that six villas were suddenly full but up until that evening the resort had only had a few guests. The guys came over from reception but I was a bit hysterical when reporting my robbery as it had really hit me that while I lay there asleep, there were some unknown people taking stuff from under the bed where I slept and from beside me. That was a terrifying thought.

They had come in through the bathroom of my villa; I had forgotten to lock the bathroom door before going to sleep. In the other villas they had actually gone through the roof to rob them. Those poor people had lost all their diving gear, diving watches and other belongings. I lost in total, between money and items, around $10,000 worth. The pity of it all for me was, as I was initially supposed to leave the week earlier, all my travel insurance had run out so I could not even claim it. So that was a very sour note to leave on, not forgetting my concern for the keyboard player as the doctors had told me he was very ill.

This should have, all in all, been enough to tell me to let things go and that Bali was not for me but when I commit to something I don't go back on my word. I also really believed in this singer and felt that he alone could really make it in Australia. I wanted him to have the opportunity as he too had an ill mother who had just been in hospital. I'd also helped him along by getting him a motorbike so he could get his mama to a doctor quickly if necessary as he was the only one of the group who did not have his own transport. He too had a large family he had been taking care of for years, as his father had died in 1992. His mum had diabetes among other medical problems.

I left the band with money for studio practice and bought amplifiers for two other members; they were for their guitars as the other two members had been given the guitars I'd brought with me. I left the keyboard in the care of the singer but had not given it to anyone. You see, I quickly learned that where there is a group of people you cannot give something to only one or two or you will create extreme jealousy

between them, (Indonesian folk are very jealous of one another, sad to say), you must give to all. So now you have a better understanding why I was compelled to loan the money when I was group targeted you might say. I still had faith that they would do the right thing by me and respect what I was trying to do and achieve on their behalf.

I left to go back to Australia and prepare for my daughter's wedding as it was on the property my late husband and I owned. It's a dreamy property with willows draped along the creek at the front of our cottage and tropical gardens. There were acres of land I had to make beautiful, the garden setting which a dear friend was organising, catering to finalise and I had to contact another dear friend who was organising the marquee and so on. I had decided that after the wedding I would return to Bali to live and fulfill my commitment to the band.

My girlfriend was going to stay on at my property and take care of the place for me. I also had to prepare everything for my beautiful soul mate, Buddy our dog, to come with me as I was not going to leave him behind. He was my baby, my 56 kilogram soppy, loveable Rotti who never had an ounce of aggression towards any human or other dog. We had had him since he was six weeks old and now he was seven years old.

We had a wonderful wedding and my eldest daughter looked so beautiful. Her sister came back from New Zealand to be chief bridesmaid and she looked stunning. The garden setting for the wedding was divine; the Marquee with all the trimmings was perfect and the food absolutely scrumptious. It was a perfect day flowing into a perfect night.

Once again I packed my bags, only this time, not only my bags; I had a shipping company coming to pack all my furniture and the belongings that I would be taking with me to Bali as my girlfriend also needed to move her furniture and belongings into my place. It all happened without a hitch. I had my visa and was personally all set to go. The

cargo company did a great job and had done it all in one full day. All went like clockwork.

I was set and gave my girlfriend and my friends a big hug and said cheerio after a barbeque the day before. Friends and neighbours and, of course, my favourite travel agent chilled out with us that day.

Chapter Two

Moving To Bali – The Honeymoon Period

Chapter Two
Moving To Bali
- The Honeymoon Period

I had hired a villa for one year; it was newly built and only just completed. It was in Sanur, as I had become familiar with this area for local shopping, restaurants and general things for everyday living. It was quite expensive in comparison to others I had looked at but they were fairly exposed with no gates or walls for privacy or security of any kind. I had hired this place because it also had three outer buildings apart from the main villa. In my mind, I decided one of the buildings, which was a little guest building, would become my office and the other would be perfect to turn into a soundproof studio so the band had their own facility and freedom to practice and meet.

I had come to believe that no place was fully secure unless you had a guard 24/7 and I had not come there to feel restraint with little privacy of my every move, day or night. I had come from a farmland environment of open spaces and never needing to lock a door. Even though I had experienced the robbery at the 'securely manned resort' I decided I would just take the sensible precautions of a low profile and an awareness surrounding me.

Fortunately, the place already had some furniture so I was able to live quite comfortably until the scheduled arrival of my container within five weeks of me settling in. My beautiful buddy, my dog, arrived two days after me. He came on his flight along with his own official passbook which was organised in Jakarta in preparation for his arrival. The wonderful vet, a husband and wife team who I had met on a previous stay and another very good musician and keyboard player in the evenings, was marvellous with the professional way he had set everything up for Bo's arrival.

I couldn't wait to go to the airport to pick him up as I was already missing him terribly. It was a hilarious moment in the huge airport hangar as he was brought in on a trailer attached to a motorised cart. I could not see

him but called out his name and he responded with his homely talk. There were lots of very mucho airport guards standing around in the hangar and all were carrying their guns and batons. They opened the cage doors for my 56 kilogram Rotti to come out and suddenly there was a mass exodus of mucho guards who instantly ran as far away as they could get. My boy leapt out of the trailer and came running to me yelping and instantly rolled over for the big tummy rub that he so loved. It cracked me and the vet up and as we made our way down the corridor, security and guards moved out of the way with their eyes bulging....it was very funny.

Bo and I settled in and took it easy the first week or so, just getting used to the warm weather which I loved so much and going for walks and he enjoyed being spoiled by the band members; he became like their mascot. I had to be extremely careful about what I ate due to severe unidentified food allergies that nearly took my life three times back home. I carried an Epi pen injection everywhere with me but at that stage only I knew how to use it. The food in Bali and anywhere in Indonesia is heavily spiced. I loved the food but it was a risk eating it. I could not touch Balinese food heavily laced with chilli that sets your throat and everything else on fire.

It was now time to pay serious attention to the band's requirements. I paid for the studio to be converted into a soundproof room as I lived between villas. In hindsight I should have just left them practicing at the local studios as I now had to purchase full band equipment including a full sound system, microphones, stands, amps and another keyboard as they decided the one I originally brought over (on recommendation from a specialist music shop in Australia) did not totally suit their needs. Mmmm....!!! So now we had two keyboards and a full drum kit; everything was genuine USA equipment. If they were going to be number one, then the gear had to be up there too.

I set up phone lines and all that I needed in my office. The studio was all rigged out with soundproofing and we were set to rock 'n roll. The band was very excited.

They came three times a week for two or three hours on Mondays, Wednesdays and Fridays. Sometimes they were all on time but other days there would be something that came up or someone would have to leave early but generally at the start they were all into it. I had set them up with a coffee station, snacks, soft drinks, water and sometimes beer. When they finished practice I would normally give them more fulfilling snacks so that they could relax and discuss music or whatever. They proudly wore their T-shirts to practice which was nice to see.

I had purchased a good car which was only one year old and had good mileage on the clock. Its bodywork was straight, which was rare for Bali with the crazy driving and drivers on the roads. It needed to be a vehicle that I could fit all the band members into when we were going to perform at a resort or restaurant so I had bought a Blazer. It was on par with Australian prices so there was not much saving there.

Several weeks had gone past and there was no word about my cargo which was supposed to have arrived in Bali and been brought to the villa as I had paid in Australia for door to door delivery. It was already past the due date, so the singer and I went and tracked down the Bali agent. When I got there I was informed that my cargo was being held in Surabaya, Java.

This news far from pleased me and then even worse than that, I was told that I would not be able to get my cargo as I didn't have the right visa. I replied that I had a multi entrant business visa. They informed me that I needed a KITAS visa which is a temporary resident visa and for that you had to have a sponsor to be there. Holy hell, what was I going to do? I had to get a sponsor. Somehow, I don't remember now, but I was given the name of an Indonesian guy who does this. We made an appointment to see this person the following day.

I was informed, once again, that I needed a KITAS visa and that my visa was no good, and then it got worse. He said that with my multi entrant visa I could not work in Bali either. Say what???....I thought, but I was cut short, "No, your visa means you can come here to set up and

buy goods and take them back to your country but you must not work here. So now you must put away your business cards and not give them out or you will be in trouble." I was stunned. I said, "But what about my cargo? I was told I will lose all my belongings." He told me many western people do lose their container of goods as they refuse to pay off customs to have it released or they give up after several months of trying to get their cargo. I was sitting there in disbelief, trying to contain myself.

He said he could change my visa but he did not do KITAS or sponsor people. However, he suggested I change to this other arrangement in the meantime, for a fee, but it was only good for 12 weeks. I thought I had no choice so paid him the money to organise it. He said that if I paid him money and gave money for him to approach the customs officers, he would go and talk to customs in Java as he was going there within days. What do you do when your hands are tied and you know they have got you? I handed over the money he had suggested would pave the way.

Though I had paid him for a short visa I still had to find a sponsor to get Kitas. This cost big money to arrange including paying to get a work visa with a woman who did this for expats and a trip to Singapore to receive my kitas visa.

We returned to my villa. I felt sick to my stomach because that container had not only my life in it, but it was of irreplaceable sentimental value. Let me explain so that you can understand me a little better, I owe it to you as you have kindly purchased my story.

What had cemented my decision to make the move to Bali, apart from my commitment to the band and their families, was that the singer and I were becoming more than just manager/singer friends. The year before going to Bali for the first time I had just experienced the worst part of my life. I had tragically lost my dearly beloved husband of 17 years. He was my soul mate, my best friend and the love of my life.

After yet another massive 'pay off' to customs in Java including further trucking to my door. Finally, my cargo arrived and I could now get organised and settle down. Things were going smoothly and the band got a couple of bookings at some new venues to kick-start their career. I had sent out letters to all the major resorts throughout Bali and had meetings with several food and beverage managers.

After much research, I prepared to go to the government to apply for them to be the first ever registered band in Bali. This would also give them status in Java and Jakarta. We made an appointment and took along a few T-shirts that I had made locally but with the same print on it stating the band's name. They always enjoy receiving gifts. The meeting went very well to the point where they wanted to hear the band play at a restaurant. At one of the popular spots back there I had organised to do a lunch and allow the band to use the restaurant to perform for the government officials. I knew that when they heard them they would get the registration. It was all set, until the keyboard player refused to do it. I don't know to this day why he did that; he just said it went against his values or some such thing. None of us were happy about this as the one opportunity was blown. I also needed the band to do this so that they were on the Indonesian's professional list of entertainers for the documents to get them into Australia.

I felt like I was banging my head up against a brick wall at every turn I made.

Six intelligence police arrived at my door one morning to arrest me as a criminal because I had given out my business card before I had my Kitas visa. They said I had to pay 25 million rupiah or go to prison for one year. I said I had Kitas just had to go to collect it, and besides I was not receiving any money working with this band quite the opposite. It made no difference to them On my return from Singapore two days later they came again with the court document and said I must go to justice the next day. After a hellish two hours of negotiations between me, them and my sponsor I had to pay 10 million there and then or go to prison. Someone (I have my suspicions who) had given my card to the police through jealousy of what I was doing to help the band and locals.

The pay out was arranged by my sponsor which I never did receive a receipt for the payment !!.

Now, all this time I was supporting the five families to help them but five families does not mean just each band member, it means the entire family. I was not only giving them all an equal amount every month but also paying for doctors, bike breakdowns, phone cards, schooling, shoes, dentists, pharmacy medicines, studio photos, outings for the group to restaurants and hotels they didn't frequent, looking for work. Each time it would mean not just drinks but also meals. The list goes on.

The next thing, I got robbed again. I had been working late in the office and was asleep on the verandah, on the lounge suite. It was around 1.30 in the morning when suddenly there was this huge roaring noise followed by the entire building shaking and rattling. I knew it was an earthquake because we had drills at school for them in my home country (where I was born); they occurred from time to time in those days.

I was really afraid and yelling. I quickly shut down my laptop which I kept padlocked to my desk, padlocked the door and ran to the verandah. Hass was still fast asleep. Suddenly I felt sick and drowsy so I climbed into the chair and went to sleep. Hass woke me around 3am and said I should go inside, so I retreated indoors with Bo, who always sleeps by my side. In the morning I was awoken by Hass and the worker who had just arrived. It was around 9am.

They said, "You must come and see." Confused at what they were saying, I followed them to the workers room, which he used daily during breaks (of which he had many). He was a friend of Hass and his family in Kupang, another island. Hass suggested I should have someone to do work and chores around the place. This was something I was very uncomfortable with as I have two hands, legs and feet and was used to looking after a house and thirteen acres of land even while working. However, it is an expected thing to employ locals, so I thought I had better not rock the boat. He was paid at a rate suggested by Hass as I didn't have a clue what they earned. It turned out, as I learnt only

about a year ago, that what I was paying him way back in 2004 is what workers get paid now.

I went to his little room and they said, "Look, someone broke in, his stuff is everywhere and a mess." He started putting things back in place but I said, "No, don't touch it, I want to call the police." They said, "There is more, come to the office." I was confused because as I passed the office to go to his room the door was still padlocked. "What is the problem, the door is still bolted?" I replied. "Come, come," and we went to the side of the office which faced the front of the villa. There it was, a panel of glass from the tiny window, complete with its timber frame, lay neatly on the grass. It was undamaged! "How the hell," I asked, "did they get through that?" I am small but would have trouble getting in there especially with the desk in the way.

I got the key and we went inside. My laptop was gone; the security wire was still attached to the desk and the security number wasn't on the dial. The office was a mess; they had gone through everything and just thrown it all over the floor. "Call the police now, please."

I was seething with fury and let out several explicit four letter words. How many police do you think turned up? At the last robbery there were about six or eight. I could not believe my eyes when they just kept coming through the gate. In total, I counted 26. Talk about contaminating a crime scene! They were anywhere and everywhere. My darling dog was acting really weirdly; I had never seen him looking so frightened and silent. He just hid under the table on the verandah all day long and would not eat or drink. He had not barked at all in those two hours or so before sunrise when this must have happened. Remember, I didn't go to bed until 3am.

The police took fingerprints from the little room and its window, the glass lying on the grass and throughout the office. One officer came over, saying they could not pull any prints off the glass as the overnight dew had made it too difficult. It was then that they said they could

bring in a tracker dog. I thought 'good luck' as there were at least 30 sets of footprints combining all the officers at the scene, the Balinese owners, myself, Hass and the worker as well as curious neighbourhood locals who always turned up in droves at any police scene going on anywhere but would not say anything to them even if they had seen the perpetrators.

Another officer came up to me and said if we brought in a dog it would cost 300,000 Rupiah. I smirked and said, "I am sure," but under my breath I said, 'What's new?' "Yes, okay." The dog just wandered around, obviously thrown by the number of scents everywhere. They took the dog out onto my driveway and little gravel roadway but as I had figured, nothing would be the outcome.

I spent most of the day serving coffee, tea and biscuits. They were there for hours, the majority just hanging out and chatting over their beverages.

The irony of the day was, once they had all left, I decided to have a quiet smoke and coffee which I had placed on the table on the verandah. Lo and behold, one of the policemen obviously took a fancy to my special cigarette lighter, which was not only an expensive purchase but it had my name beautifully engraved on it, as it was gone! That had really pissed me right off. This is the thing with many Indonesian people, I'm sorry to say. They smile at you, engage you in polite conversation and then get you from behind. I was exhausted but then had to clean up after serving food and drink all day. In the evening there was a knock at the gate and standing there were three intelligence police. 'Oh boy, what now?' I wondered. They were very polite and wished to go over the robbery quietly and with me alone. Thank goodness they spoke good English. They noted down answers I gave to their questions and then they asked, "How come you keep getting robbed? We saw in the Police files that you have been robbed before." I gave a reply stating that I didn't have a clue.

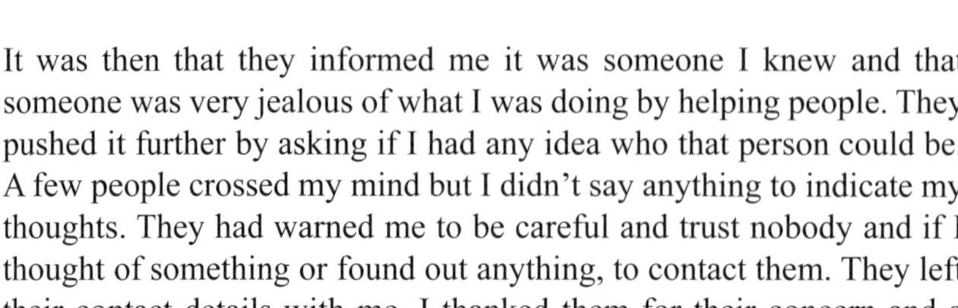

It was then that they informed me it was someone I knew and that someone was very jealous of what I was doing by helping people. They pushed it further by asking if I had any idea who that person could be. A few people crossed my mind but I didn't say anything to indicate my thoughts. They had warned me to be careful and trust nobody and if I thought of something or found out anything, to contact them. They left their contact details with me. I thanked them for their concern and a short time later they left.

I was very distraught about losing my laptop as I had very few files backed up on CD and my life was in that computer, including my work back in Australia and everything I had done with the band. Programs, letters, emails and banking details were in there too so all this was of grave concern to me. Later in the week I went with a distant relative of the singer, to purchase a desktop computer as he was a technician and knew could the best places to go so I could get the better brands at a good price. I had no insurance, so once again was out of pocket. I thought, 'If you want to come back in a few weeks to steal from me again I am going to make it bloody difficult for you sods.' As much as I would have preferred another laptop, it just was not practical.

I settled down to a quiet evening and, feeling quite numb, discussed the robbery with Hass. He thought that with what had happened it would be best if he stayed the night to make sure I was safe. We spent many hours out on the verandah just talking. He told me, like before, that I must not go anywhere without him and to trust nobody. I lived by my motto of trust even though I had become a target several times in different ways. It would be difficult for me to be someone I wasn't but I understood what he was saying and it was also what the police had said to me and they had no attachment to me in any way.

I had an argument with the worker the next day as he'd done something to hide the fact that he had broken Hass's motorbike. I bought the motorbike for Hass before leaving the first time so that he had transport for his mother. I was angry at the worker as he rode the bike like a gangster and was dangerous on the roads. Then I found out he had

approached the Balinese owners of my villa to borrow money from them and he snuck away to get the bike fixed without excusing himself or asking if he could leave work, and believe me, he had a very cushy job. Unlike most villa workers, he did very little each day. I told him off, so then he got angry and would not talk to me at first after which, he sat there crying. I told him I would need him to stay on that evening while we went to a venue the band was playing at, especially in light of the robbery the previous day. He refused and said he was going home at five. This really made me mad. You see, not only was he being paid top brass for working at my place but the place he called home was Hass's mama's little house which I also paid for, including the food and electricity and they told me he gave no money for rent. I tried again but he refused and just sat by the pool. It was then that I decided his days were numbered, no matter how unpopular I may become but I would keep it to myself until the end of the month when he got paid.

The band returned later in the afternoon to get equipment ready for their performance. Well, did the worker give a story and a half! Not that I understood anything he had said, as they talked in their home dialect of Kupang. Then Hass got angry with me and questioned me about why I told the worker I had bought the bike for him. I had nothing to hide as the band knew I had bought it and I was unaware it was some kind of deep secret. I was not used to the game of Indonesia that was played. I am a simple girl, open and honest. All was well, even though this just added fuel to the fire and opened my eyes to the fact that this worker had no respect for me and I could not trust him. I was paying his wages so why should I be questioned? Now I knew for sure that this guy had to go and I would not hire another person, male or female, to assist me with anything.

I didn't like the fact that he watched my every move, glance or word anyway and reported everything I did. This was bullshit. Fortunately, I did not have to do the nasty deed of firing him as he decided to leave at the end of the month. What a huge relief for me. Now maybe I could return to being myself without tip toeing around and feeling like I was the one being employed. My steep learning curve was just beginning.

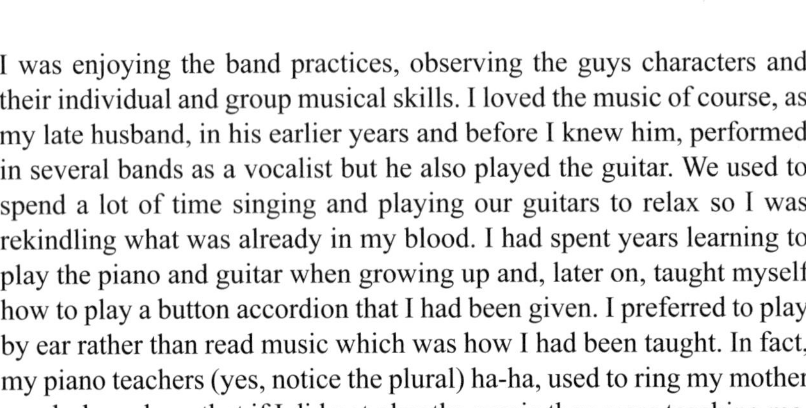

I was enjoying the band practices, observing the guys characters and their individual and group musical skills. I loved the music of course, as my late husband, in his earlier years and before I knew him, performed in several bands as a vocalist but he also played the guitar. We used to spend a lot of time singing and playing our guitars to relax so I was rekindling what was already in my blood. I had spent years learning to play the piano and guitar when growing up and, later on, taught myself how to play a button accordion that I had been given. I preferred to play by ear rather than read music which was how I had been taught. In fact, my piano teachers (yes, notice the plural) ha-ha, used to ring my mother regularly and say that if I did not play the music they were teaching me, then they could no longer be my teacher. You see, I can listen to a song and pick it up instantly and play it. The band never knew this about me, nor that could I play a button accordion. I had been writing song lyrics and poetry for a long time.

Okay, back to my story.

Chapter Three

Reality Hits Home – Honeymoon Over

Chapter Three
Reality Hits Home – Honeymoon Over

Things were going along smoothly during the month until one day when band practice had just started and Hass received a phone call to say his sister, who he really loved and who lived on another island, had suddenly died a couple of hours ago. Of course, he came to me in utter shock and told me what had happened. He said he would have to go to Kupang straight away but would I come with him first to tell his mama. We had already moved his mama twice, upgrading on each occasion to a bigger and better house. Now I had paid for her to live in a large house as his sister's young daughters were living with her. I had been told a story about his sister and why they were there. It disturbed me that the house I'd rented for her and the children had turned into a 'come one, come all.' When we arrived there the house was full of these free-loaders. Hass had made frantic calls to his brother, who had his own home with his own family, asking him to come to the house while we told Mama the dreadful news. She wondered why we had all turned up at once. The band had gone home but Hass and I had arranged with the keyboard player that he, his wife and daughters would stay to look after my villa and Bo my dog which, thank goodness, they loved.

Hass had asked me if I would go with him to this other island to bury his sister. I knew this was going to be really tough for me as I was, in all honesty, still raw about the sudden death of my late husband, even though nearly two years had passed. However, I was feeling his distress and pain so I said yes. I also knew he had no money for airfares or the other things that were ahead.

It was awful sitting there when his mama was told the news. It did not sink in when he told her the first time and he had to repeat it. The painful sound coming from deep within her was devastating to witness. The two little girls also had to be told and that was crippling as they had already lost their daddy.

We packed a quick bag as Hass had managed to get us on a flight within two hours. He asked me to take my video camera because he told his mama he was taking me with him and that I would film everything for her and the family. Oh God, on hearing this I tried to pull my strength together without showing the sheer panic which was welling up inside me. I had no idea what lay ahead, all I knew was that I was not only going to an island I had not visited before but I was also going into Hass's childhood and family stamping ground, which was strict Muslim territory. On the flight, Hass came clean about his sister. He had borrowed money from me some time back saying his sister needed it for something. What he revealed to me on the plane shocked me. His sister was actually in prison and that was why he had borrowed money from me; he had been attempting to buy her out.

From what he had been told on the phone, when someone rang from Kupang to say she was dead, they had just finished their visit with her and one minute she was alive, the next she was dead. They said she came out of the chief's office in the prison, assisted by two officers, and then she had screamed out to them, "I wish I was dead," and within about ten minutes she really was dead. This was like a horror movie.

We were met off the plane by some of his cousins and aunty.

Hass told me we had to go to the morgue as the police were doing an autopsy on her which was just over the road from the prison.

My mind had so many things flashing through it as we sped to the mortuary. I was feeling ill inside and also panicking about whether my clothes were right for going into the unknown Muslim community. We pulled up at this really depressing little concrete block building. He asked me to get the camera out. Several people were sitting outside on the grass and turned out to be family and close friends of Hass and his sister. They gave me a friendly greeting. I shot a little bit of footage but felt most uncomfortable intruding in this way with people grieving and in shock. Hass made some more painful phone calls to family on the island.

It was ghastly and daunting to sit there listening to the sounds of saws and a drill coming from inside the building. I kept getting up and walking around but there was nowhere to go to get away from it. I was amazed to observe these people carrying on quite normally as though nothing had happened or was happening; I was not witnessing anyone in a state of grief, at least outwardly. I think I was more upset than they were, physically at least.

In my mind I went through the past few months since I'd arrived in Indonesia and could not believe what I had been confronted with in such a short period of time. It was mind boggling to say the least. This was not normal life as I knew it to be or should be. I was beginning to understand what 3rd world country meant. My innocence and naivety was being rapidly stripped away and replaced with inconceivable, factual, stark reality. There were no fancy frills covering up the hardship or sorrow; I was living right in amongst it. It was in my face.

Even though I was an earthy spiritual person my thoughts were simple, my education basic, I had never lived the high life but that is not to say I didn't enjoy some luxuries on occasion. I had experienced those things when working in the film and television industry and travelling and staying in five star accommodation when we and the crew were away on an exotic island filming, for example. But on the overall scale of things, self importance and pumping up ones ego to stand out had never impressed me. I had already lived life and experienced more than most ever would in their lifetime.

My thoughts were abruptly interrupted when Hass came hurrying over and said that we had to go inside, now. I was looking around as we went inside but my instincts were telling me, prepare yourself girl, here we go. My breathing intensified as we stood outside the room in which his sister was lying dead. My head was screaming, 'I can't do this; please don't ask me to go in there.' Then I heard his voice saying, come on now, we're going in and I want you to film it! Oh shit, oh God, no, but before I knew it I was standing in this awful, sinister, grey concreted room and there before my eyes lay his sister. Whoops, sorry, I need to

take a break for a moment; I still cry when I tell the story or even think about it....back in a minute.

Okay, this is hard but I will continue. Here was this lovely looking woman lying naked on a concrete bed. The floors were flooded with water. The police morticians were washing down the instruments they'd used during the autopsy. What a ghastly sight and place. It was like a movie depicting the olden days, going back to the turn of the century. I had to film Hass's sister lying there, to show his mama when we returned to Bali. How could we show her this? This was the child that she had brought into the world twenty something years before. The next thing, there was panic in the room as they moved her grayish, purple body onto a type of stretcher. I was wondering how in hells name they were going to get her out of the room onto the stretcher as she was a large framed woman and quite tall. You see their father was not Indonesian, he was born in the Netherlands; their mother was Indonesian. When Hass's father was alive he was the head of the Timor Leste police. He was a large, very tough and solid man over six feet tall.

They struggled to manoeuvre the sister's body firstly onto the stretcher and then it was a dramatic struggle to get it through the door. Once outside in the covered area of the building they quickly lowered her to the concrete floor where Hass bent over his sister said something to her and kissed her on the cheek. My hands were trembling while I was trying to film this and tears were rolling down my face, as they are now. I used to lay elderly folk out years ago when I worked in the aged care hospital but nothing ever affected me like this except my own family members who have died.

They placed this metal cradle type of top over her which was not solid; there were gaps between the joins on this thing. They then placed a green cotton type of material over the top of the cradle and immediately picked her up and rushed her towards the waiting vehicle. It wasn't a hearse like Westerners have for transporting a corpse to a funeral.

We jumped in someone's car and all the vehicles sped through the streets towards the village where the service was being held. You see, being Muslim, a person must be buried within hours of the death and time had already been lost because of the autopsy. To this day, neither Hass nor his family have been given any explanation of the cause or reason for her death.

We entered the narrow streets, which were like a maze, heading to the house where the service was being held. The cars stopped well short of the house as the street, like standard tradition for any kind of ceremony whether it is Indonesian or Balinese-Indonesian, was blocked off. I gazed up the street we were hastily walking along to see a sea of people and chairs in the street with many women sitting there. Now I felt complete intimidation; fearful me being this strange white woman and to top it off, a video camera in her hand, filming. I wanted to run in the opposite direction but knew I must see this through for the sake of Hass's mama and family.

We went inside and Hass said to keep filming. A sea of eyes was on me. I was trying to breathe; I wanted and needed a cigarette so badly. My nerves were shattered. I met another brother who was living in Kupang. He was also very large framed and towered over my 5'2" insignificant frame. I was ushered into a room by Hass but I didn't know what was behind that door. He opened it and told me to go in and film. I found myself standing there in close quarters with several very busy Muslim ladies. Sis was laid out there and they were washing her body down, preparing her to be taken to the cemetery. Hass came in and once again leaned over his beautiful sister. This was more than I could bear to witness let alone film. My hands were shaking so much they had become uncontrollable for a moment. I was weeping as I watched him say his final goodbye to her through the lens. His brother then came in and did the same but he broke down crying. Women were crying and wailing. Sis was then moved again to another room where they dressed her as she lay on the bed. They covered her in balm to prevent the odour of death.

Someone found a white garment to drape her still body in as Muslims must be buried in white cloth. A white hijab covered her beautiful, waist length, black hair. After that was complete there was a parade as all the women attending the ceremony said their sorrowful goodbyes; all the time I was rolling the camera. I had never met his sister until now and was so sad that this was my introduction and farewell at the same time.

We never got to share a moment, which I would have loved. Apparently she was larger than life in her personality and she stood up, not only to authority but to anyone who challenged her. She was adored by many but those who resented this strong woman had been party to her demise. We were of the firm belief that she had met with foul play and a very unpleasant death within the jail.

I was offered something to eat as there was a banquet of food and everyone was grazing while all this was taking place. I did not comprehend this and sure as hell could not take in any food rather, I was feeling ill. I did have a cup of much needed coffee as it was part of my staple diet and I had not had one for hours.

The Imam performed the service which I also had to film. Now everyone knew who I was as news travels very quickly. I went outside with the majority of people once they had again transferred Hass's sister back onto this stretcher bed with the cradle placed over her. Several prayers were said once they got her out the door and a group of men had to hold her above their heads. They were struggling to hold their position as she was a big lady and most of the men were only about 5'1" or 5'2". They moved a little further forward and another special prayer was said. They were at the top of several steps and Hass and his brother were in the front on either side of her. His brother was overcome with grief and I could see he was fast losing his grip. I, like everyone else, could see this and had started to let out a gasp as he started to sway to the side; we all had the same thought going through our minds - if he drops her, OMG I don't know what will happen.

It was very close; he was off balance and about to fall down when, thank God, another man quickly grabbed that side of the stretcher. My eye was intensely focused down the lens of the camera but my mind was blank. Before I knew what was happening they were down the stairs, had turned to the left and they were on a full flight march up the street with everyone following behind them at a fast pace. I almost had to run to keep up with them and had no idea what was happening or where they were headed; was it the cemetery or what? It became clear as I rounded the bend which they had taken before I got there as I could not get past the mass of people in order to catch up.

I saw the mosque out of the corner of my eye. It was off to the right and they, that is only the men, had entered the grounds. I panicked, knowing I could not enter as you must wear white prayer clothing which you don't put on until you have bathed to cleanse yourself first. It's like you see on television; hands, face, ears and feet must be washed to enter the mosque. A girl was giving me an aggressive look saying something to me and doing hand signals telling me not to enter. I had no intention of going in as I understood the Muslim rules. Thank goodness some guy took my camera and off he went.

They soon returned carrying Sis out again. I thought, 'Oh please let her have peace soon.' We were off again, this time to the cemetery. We pulled up on the roadside and walked a little then we were climbing up this hard clay hillside. I thought, 'What? Is this the cemetery? It can't be.' But sure enough, at the top of the steep climb it lay pitifully before me.

What a sad place and environment to be laid to rest; on a hill of sheer, hard, rocky, brown clay. Men were just finishing off digging the grave and were still standing at the bottom of the hole. I heard myself gasp and tears once again fell down my cheeks. I was muttering a prayer to myself saying, 'Please Allah, take this woman to rest in peace and watch over her.' Everyone was chatting around me like they were taking a stroll in the park.

The Imam said prayers over her and Hass was on the other side from me signalling for me to film. All I wanted to do was pray for her. The hole seemed to be about twenty feet down. Men then struggled to carry the body down where they laid Sis on the clay earth. When you stand there and physically see this it is far different from viewing it on television. The feeling of emotion overwhelms you and when they place a piece of cardboard over the body, even knowing this is the Muslim way, it is very hard to come to terms with. I didn't handle it well and burst out crying. They then proceeded to shovel the clay on top of her and fill the grave in.

It was all more than I could bear. I was then taken by Hass to see her husband's grave; another pitiful sight, no headstone, just a simple little cross was all that represented him. How sad, so very, very daunting. We left not long after that and checked in at a hotel. We were shattered by grief and the witnessing of yet another unnecessary death; a family member cut down in the prime of her life leaving two beautiful little girls behind, one aged 2 and the other 4.

To this day, nobody has ever been given an answer for her death or told how it was caused. The family never received a death certificate. It was like she was totally irrelevant to officials as a human being and one who was loved by a family. Who or what was being covered up?

It horrified me, the callousness and cold treatment of a human life; like people arc just another number. People are afraid to rock the boat and ask questions, even though it is their democratic right.

We visited a few of Hass's family in town as he had not seen many of them for years and they wanted to know how his mama was. It was arranged that we would be picked up and driven to the area, a two or three hour drive away, where he spent his childhood. It was nice travelling through the countryside and great for him to see the different places he'd grown up in and visited. It was a long trip as the roads were second grade with an ever-changing landscape and terrain to travel over.

We met up with close family and they welcomed me warmly. There was much giggling and chatter from all parts of the room. Hass wanted to go and visit the graveyard in the village where his baby brother had died at around thirteen months of age. The stories he'd shared with me since I got to know him, were totally heart-rending.

We gathered some flowers from the garden and bottles of water to take with us to clean his little gravesite. Oh how sad; here lay the tiny grave of his baby brother.

We cleaned all around the gravesite and the top of it; following the tradition of laying the flower petals and sprinkling water on the top. I watched and followed Hass and the few family members his age also contributed in the process. Hass said a prayer over him which by now caused my emotions to become a flood of tears. I had to walk away and find space for myself to come to terms with everything because most day to day living is so matter of fact in Indonesia. The saying they use so often is, 'That's life.' I used to find that one difficult to swallow as it is used to explain away or accept just about anything.

We had a long journey to return to the hotel that day. I was both physically and emotionally drained. Hass asked if I could contribute some money towards the funeral as it was the community that had organised it. "Of course," I said, knowing it would not have looked good if he had not put something towards it. We returned to Bali a day or so later.

I was not looking forward to taking this footage back for the family to view as it was so graphic and very upsetting to watch. The family gathered the following day at Hass's mama's house. It was gut-wrenching to sit and see the pain on Mama's face. She also wanted to know everything. There was little he could tell her and he certainly wasn't able to give her closure or understanding about why or how she had died. I just continued to cry while watching the footage that I'd shot; it was like reliving the day's events all over again.

Things went back to normal fairly quickly. I was glad to be home and back to the comfort of my loyal dog. Band practice resumed, although the first day was taken up with reporting the recent events.

About a month or two later, Hass told me he needed to go to another island as his brother was getting married; the one from Kupang. As the head of the family, Hass needed to be a witness. I felt a little uneasy as this meant no band practice for a few of the scheduled sessions. I was surprised that he wanted to go the following day but he needed an airline ticket and a hotel room. Once again, I assisted him with money.

The next day, the band showed up for practice. They wondered why he was late and then I realised he hadn't told any members of the band that he was going. After telling them he'd gone and why, they went to the studio. I continued doing things in the villa but about ten minutes later they all came to the verandah and said they wanted to have a meeting with me. It was like a showdown with the drummer; the one who had not only borrowed the large sum of money for his wife but two other amounts as well.

He was aggressive and demanding about the band to the point of altercation. These guys had received total flexibility so that if they did not have a gig on they were free to play with other groups as long as they let me know. The others allowed him to lead the attack on me, which included putting Hass down.

I was devastated and did not appreciate what was being said in its full context and felt they had little, and in his case, no respect for me at all. They left soon after that. I was totally distraught and contacted Hass. He said he would sort it out when he got back. I spent a lot of time crying. The meeting was to be held at the keyboard player's home. I took the contracts that were going to be cancelled with me as they needed to sign them. On the way, Hass had said to me I should just cancel the contracts but not ask about the money they owed. I asked why, but he didn't answer my question.

On sitting down I took a deep breath and listened. Choked up, I agreed to them disbanding. There was nothing I could do or say and I figured that as they had unanimously decided this, there was no point in trying to convince them not to. I was taken aback when the instigator jumped up and came around to peck me on the cheek, smiling from ear to ear and saying thank you. I found out much later, as in a year or so, that he had then gone to some government department to report me. I don't know what about nor the particular department but he was told by my sponsor, who was friends with him in their church, that he should drop what he was attempting to do against me as he would not only lose but it would also cost him a lot of money (which he had none of) and it could take years to have anything done. She actually confirmed to me that he had done this. What a double whammy shock for me.

So it was done and dusted, everything that I had invested in these guys and doing whatever it took to produce these guys at the highest level as musicians, including selling my wonderful property in Australia, was gone. It took me years to get over that and even now, mature musicians in Bali still talk about the band. Hass went back to regular solo and lectern singing at different resorts and restaurants.

I had moved as I did not want to pay the high rate for the villa again. I found a comfortable house just up the road from Hass's mama's place at a much reduced contract price for a year. I had now bought 10 are (1/4 acre of land) with Hass being my voluntary nominee so that I could do this. I had special legal documents from the lawyer which gave me complete power of attorney over the property.

Later that year my sponsor wanted to meet me for coffee. This was unusual, I thought, as we had never done this in all the time I knew her. With pleasantries done on our greeting she informed me she could no longer be my sponsor when it came up for renewal, which was only a short time away. Hass had come with me for some reason. She suggested that if he and I were married, he could be my sponsor. It surprised me that she would get into our private relationship. I said I

would never marry someone just to allow me to live in a country. I would look around for another sponsor and I would be in touch. We left and I was feeling daunted by my situation of having to find another sponsor but I knew of a few agents that sponsored several Westerners. Many advertised in the paper but you had to be careful and word of mouth was normally a better source to investigate first.

I think it was more because it had come without any hint or warning that it caught me off guard but it was achievable so I was not overly stressed by her not being able to sponsor me the following year.

Hungry, we stopped at a café and that is when Hass asked me if I would like to be married to him. Straight away I said, "You don't have to do that because I cannot just marry someone. If it is not love then I can't." He said he had wanted to ask me for some time and even when we were in Kupang for his sister's funeral he had rung his childhood sweetheart and told her he was going to get married. I didn't know this but I wanted to make sure before I gave him an answer as I hadn't been expecting him to pop the question. He said he had already discussed marrying me with his mama.

Knowing that Muslims marry to reproduce sounds crass but in Indonesia, you get married and people wait for the first baby to arrive on the scene. I had to be sure he fully understood that I could never conceive a child due to having to have a hysterectomy when I was just twenty seven years old. If that is what he had hoped for by marrying someone then I was not going to rob him of this opportunity. He convinced me that he never thought he would ever marry and this was God's gift to him and it did not bother him if he did or didn't have children. He said love and communication were more important to him.

We got on amazingly well and communicated easily with so much in common. There was a notable difference in our ages as far as crunching the numbers went but there was no difference in our relationship and no gaps on any level. Our intimacy was incredibly inseparable and sensual. Our relationship was strong and meaningful. We laughed a lot and had

fun together. We sang and danced like children. We were very attentive to each other's needs. We cooked together, he taught me his culture and likewise I taught him western culture. We just wanted a simple life, peaceful, happy and to help others where it was possible for us to do so.

I had studied the holy Quran after I returned to Australia from my first trip and from what I learned, the pure thesis of Islam (over all other religions) appeared to me at that time, to have the structure of how I tried to live my life and be a good person on a daily basis, no matter what I was doing, or with whom. I have never been racially prejudiced and raised my own children the same way.

In the end and over a long period of time I found I did not comprehend some of the teachings and I became very confused. The reality of a lot of interpretations, as I observed in a number of the Muslim people who I met, was far different from the holy Quran in its pure written form. Later in the book you will understand what I am saying here so bear with me. I also had to remember that no matter what religion people are, everyone is an individual and each one interprets their religion differently and acts upon that. Some, like in any religion, are outright hypocrites and this is what drove me from entering any church building. I just followed 'God' wherever I was and I was always very happy and comfortable this way.

Hass asked me again if I would marry him and this time I said, "Yes."

The Indonesian government had changed some laws as they were trying to stomp out all the illegal marriages between Western and Indonesian people, mainly men. It was very stressful organising everything as there were many documents that had to be prepared and acquired. My sponsor said she would organise the legal side of it as men would often take Indonesian women as their wives in illegal ceremonies just so that they could get to stay in Indonesia. Many Indonesian men also had several illegal wives and used agents to perform the ceremonies for a price. This is still the case, even with the changed laws and national registration IDs in place to try to stop it. Many wives don't know about

the other woman and in some cases it is the reverse. They can never have a legal marriage certificate or the marriage book that is given unless a marriage ceremony is done legally.

Being a western woman, I had to have permission (even at my age) from my brother and other family members stating, in writing, that they gave consent to my marriage. Oh my Lord! This had to be sent not only to the authorities in Jakarta but also to the Governor General of my country of origin. As time was running out on my current KITAS visa things had to move quickly. It all had to happen within a month. Documents were going back and forth from country to country with approvals and permissions and we also had to organise the wedding ceremony and prepare and set in motion an application for my new visa and status which meant that straight after the wedding I would once again have to go offshore to receive my new visa for temporary residence.

My head was in a spin. The easiest part was the wedding ceremony. It was going to be in the large Mosque in Denpasar after prayers at 7pm. Hass had said he did not want a big flashy wedding due to having no money. I respected that and as I had no friends there and it would be difficult for any friend or family member to come from Australia, there was little point. I was surprised though, as he had so many friends and I felt sure he would want to invite a few close ones. But no, it was just going to be his mama and her sister who was staying with her at the time, his brother and two other couples; family and friends of Hass and his mama.

A Muslim government official was appointed to represent me and witness the marriage on my behalf as I had no brother or parent attending as they were dead. In one way I felt a bit sad but then I had been to many Indonesian weddings where many people came to the feast and then left. This costs a fortune and is usually held in a hotel or resort venue and it is very glamorous. Those that can't afford this will usually have it in someone's house but once again, many people come but there is no personal interaction between the guests and the bridal couple. The ceremony takes place, they eat and they leave. The difference between them is quite extreme.

Hass and I went to find an outfit for me to wear. We decided on white pants with a matching dress top and a nice scarf to cover my head. It was simple but stylish without making a statement. The day arrived. Hass had planned to take me and his mama to the hairdresser. He did not say what was going on or why but just told her we would pick her and his aunty up at six o'clock that night. Once we got inside the Mosque he told his mama we were there to get married.

My sponsor also came and sat alongside me during the ceremony. I had given her a million rupiah to purchase special ceremonial food to hand out to whoever was at the Mosque for prayer that night. After the marriage she had tears of joy on her face. After the ceremony we ate downstairs before returning to our house with our few family and friends to cut the stunning wedding cake we had made. It was three layers. The next day Hass sent a text message to the old band members saying that we had married and they were welcome to come to our house to share some food and cake. Only one couple came.

We took off for Australia a week and a bit later to complete my new visa which would be the wife KITAS temporary resident visa. It would have to be renewed each year for the next six years but I no longer had to go offshore to process it. In the seventh year (that was back then, now a new law has made it two years) I would then receive the KITAP visa, which you don't have to renew for five years. This is the current law. Once you receive your new visa you must report to police headquarters to register it and if you don't do that within thirty days of receiving your visa you can be fined up to 10 million rupiah or more and you run the risk of being a guest in the infamous jail in Bali.

I had arranged with my son in-law, as the timing was perfect for my daughter's birthday, that we would come to stay and surprise her as her birthday gift. When we arrived we snuck around the side of their home. He had told her she should cook a roast lamb dinner (my favourite) as friends from his work were coming for dinner. He made sure that she was out on the back patio with him so that she couldn't hear or see the car when we arrived.

It worked out perfectly! I stuck my head around the corner and said "Happy birthday." She shrieked so loudly that her neighbours rang, thinking something serious had happened. I took Hass into Brisbane to the main mall area and we had a meal to die for. It was at my suggestion; steaks and king prawns from one of my favourite places in the mall. Well, a couple of times after that, Hass asked if we could go there again. So it was well worth the 54 kilometre trip to see the enjoyment and delight on his face when eating this meal.

We headed up the Sunshine Coast for our honeymoon and I took him to some of my favourite rain forest and waterfall spots. We had a great time.

It took a couple of weeks for my visa to arrive but then we returned to Bali. Life was good. We were busy with music; I was writing song lyrics and he composed the music for them.

Most days were fairly normal, going about our usual chores and checking on Mama. In the evenings when Hass was singing I would go with him to the resorts or restaurants. This was my only contact with western people and a chance to have a conversation as I still had no friends in Bali. On nights when he wasn't singing we generally went to some venue so that he could chat with other muso friends. Inevitably he would be asked to get up and sing for the guests. Westerners were amazed at his voice and how he could sing any style with equal quality and performance.

We had to keep a close eye on his mama as she was diabetic and got sick very easily. She didn't like taking her medicine, which created problems, and she had already been hospitalised twice since I got to know her. It never bothered her that she was sick, which was good in one way as she never played on it, but at the same time it was detrimental because when she needed treatment it was hard to get her to understand the importance of taking care of herself. Of course, it also created unnecessary costs and outlay for doctors, hospital treatment and medication.

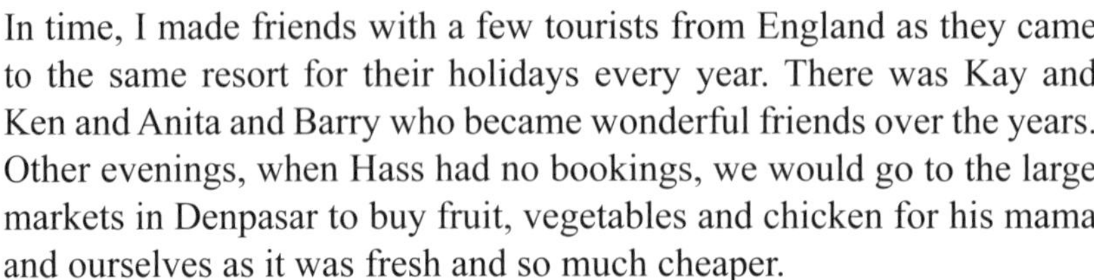

In time, I made friends with a few tourists from England as they came to the same resort for their holidays every year. There was Kay and Ken and Anita and Barry who became wonderful friends over the years. Other evenings, when Hass had no bookings, we would go to the large markets in Denpasar to buy fruit, vegetables and chicken for his mama and ourselves as it was fresh and so much cheaper.

Hass told me he used to be involved with a CB radio network years ago and so, thinking he should still have this opportunity, I purchased a new CB radio of his choice so that he could continue this hobby even though I didn't fully understand it or the people. Every now and again he would chat to people late in the evening and share their stories with me. He had a special call sign and when he called up, people seemed excited to hear his voice and would often ask him to sing a song over the CB radio.

He was happy and I was happy to see him enjoying life. He had a contagious smile.

It surprised me one day when he asked for some money to pay the annual rent for his room. The surprise was because I didn't know he still had this room, since we had been together for two years! This was the place he was living in when I first met him but I had never seen it. I had heard from various people that he was married and left a wife and two children. I asked him directly about this and he said that it was a lie and he had never been married. I trusted him and believed that this was the truth, even though I kept hearing this in the following years. Many people were saying to me, 'Be careful, we are worried for you' but at this stage I saw nothing to indicate anything other than what was before me, even though I did a little probing.

As his bed was at his mother's house I had presumed he no longer lived in his rented room as he never spoke of it until that moment. He had somehow paid for this place the year before although he wasn't working. It became one of many unanswered questions. Anyway, he paid it up and moved his belongings out of there into our place and his mama's home.

Chapter Four

The Nightmare Villa Build

Chapter Four
The Nightmare Villa Build

Having had the land for several months I thought it was time to start building plans for the villa. I wanted a design that was similar to my cottage back in Australia as it had double doors opening out onto verandahs which allowed the internal and external environment to meet as one. I love nature and tropical gardens. We sat down and as Hass had already been to my property in Australia before I sold it, he understood the basic design and liked it too. He did some rough sketches and we moved this and that around and enlarged the areas.

I wanted it to be open plan for freedom and to let the air flow in because of the humid conditions in Bali all year round. It needed to have plenty of space so that when the family came for occasions like Lebaran the Muslim feasting and holiday time after the month of Ramadan fasting everyone could relax. This is the equivalent of western society celebrating Christmas but without all the material attachments. It is about rekindling family, friendships, good wishes and forgiveness for wrong doing.

It needed, of course, to have a music studio as I still had all the band and sound equipment I'd purchased for the band but I also thought Hass would have many friends coming to jam sessions and we could make some business with the equipment. It used to frustrate me that all the musicians were and still are paid 3rd world wages at resorts and restaurants to entertain western guests. It was difficult to get bookings with resorts as the underlying habit of food and beverage managers was to negotiate the rate of pay and if you wanted to get regular group bookings at a venue you had to give an under-the-table cut to the manager or not get the bookings.

This, to me, is shameful as it takes musicians worldwide a lot of energy to entertain as they give from their soul when they perform. There are and were a lot of musicians however that just needed money and didn't

take their music too seriously. They didn't practice, often turned up late or not at all, or swapped with another muso if they got a better deal for that night. Any place that Hass sang at would pay the equivalent of between $10 and $12 dollars for a night of great entertainment. You can't live on that or pay bills. This is generally still the situation in Bali especially if you don't make sure you receive what you deserve. There are just a handful of artists receiving a higher level of pay but they too have had to negotiate that and stand their ground.

The one night a year they all hang out for is New Years Eve. They have to audition for resorts and pray that they get a good booking as on this night they are paid the equivalent of one or two months salary, depending on the resort. There is much competition to get the good venues at places like Nusa Dua, Seminyak and Kuta but even then, food and beverage managers squeeze them as much as possible. They can receive anything from $100 (1,200,000 rupiah; that is 1 million two hundred thousand rupiah) for the night to 2.5 million rupiah (250.00) per person in a group or solo artist. They don't get paid straight after the event, normally they have to wait up to a month to receive this. It is a tough industry there, like everything else. The fees have never increase much at all over the past ten years although the tourists are at there highest level ever now.

It is an extremely long day for the musicians as they must leave their homes in the morning, before the main roads are closed off in all the areas. Traffic is a nightmare at the best of times in Bali but this particular day/night is ten times worse. They must hang out at the venue all day waiting to do sound checks and be available, normally, for a 6:30pm or 7pm start, through to 1am or 2am in the morning, then travel home again. So you can see, not even this is a great deal of money for what is involved and the waiting period before they are paid.

Construction of the villa was started after my lawyer introducing us to a builder. My lawyer had grown up with Hass back in Timor-Timor (Tim-Tim) as they called it. I thought he would be trustworthy as they had history!!!!

I paid the builder an upfront payment for the building permit to get started quickly. The process contract stated that there would be interim payments and I had to pay 50% of the full contract building price up front. When I questioned this, I was told by my lawyer that it was the norm for Bali or Indonesia. I found out much later that this was not the case at all. I had to pay the interim payments at each of 5 stages.

I heard on the grapevine that I needed to pay particular attention to the project once it was underway and be there most of the time to keep an eye on everything. I took this on board as I had now heard so many stories of builders not only doing shoddy, substandard work but many cases where the builder took off with the money. This worried me to say the least as I still could not grasp the language and was at a disadvantage but I thought he would have my back as this was to be our home. Excited but nervous, the building started. We were there for the clearing of the land, which I had been lucky enough to buy at a very good price from an elderly Dutchman who had lived in Indonesia and Bali since the 1940s. It was on the Eastern side of Bali, out of the hustle and bustle of pollution and noise in the busy areas of Bali and was still natural, surrounded by local village life and only a few minutes walk onto a natural beach.

I queried many things as I knew a little about building and when I saw inadequate cement, for example, being added to the mix I made it known that this was not acceptable. I kept in mind at all times that Bali was a high risk area, like the whole of Indonesia, for strong earthquakes and tremors. It was going to be a large villa, 18 x 22 metres on two levels, so it needed to be done properly.

One day, while sitting at home watching the TV, I saw vivid footage on the news of this tsunami. I asked Hass where it was as I had not heard about the earthquake or tsunami in Ache and the other countries. I was shocked sitting there watching the horrendous pictures on the screen. I found myself instantly writing a song as tears poured down my cheeks. I said we should produce a song and donate the sales to the victims. We set about composing the music with Hass singing, of course, and

when it was ready, I said, "Okay, lets book the recording studio in the Renon area," as it had a good reputation as did the recording technician. I searched through and purchased many FX (sound effects) that could be included with the music track as I planned to do a DVD after the CD was produced.

The song is called Tsunami, Hearts That Weep with lyrics by me, Sandi Allan and vocals by my husband, music composition by him, narration by me, produced and directed by me. I did the artwork for the CD. It sounded great at the completion of the recording. I own all the copyrights to the song and hope to release it one day.

Building was progressing but then the builder wanted an advance payment on the next stage even though he had not even finished the first. The excuse given to me, with Hass translating, was that he needed it early to keep the workers there and prevent delays. I didn't think this was right as he had already had 50% plus stage one of the money. I asked my lawyer about it but ended up having to pay. To cut a long story short, this continued to happen at each stage and I knew something was not right. I expressed my concerns to Hass over and over but he took no action. Then it came time to render the walls with cement, which his workers were meant to do. Normally women do this work, not the men. The women could not do what I wanted and I tried to show them over a period of two days what the finish had to be like, even though I had never done this before. They kept doing the smooth finish you see on plaster walls but this was not what the main areas upstairs or downstairs were supposed to be like. In the end, they walked away from doing it altogether and the builder would not hire anyone else to do it.

Guess who ended up doing the lot? Little old me. Hass could not be singing six nights a week plus keep an eye on the project and watch the group of men now camping on site so I suggested to him that he needed to cut back to only two or three nights a week or he would get ill. With that, he mixed the small buckets of cement mix for me (when the women were busy and could not do it) and I applied it. It was hard going as the ceilings were twelve feet high and I don't like heights so I was challenged on every stroke I applied up high. This took me a total of twelve weeks to complete. I would do it night and day, sometimes working right through the night while Hass slept on the cement floor.

I would often buy food for the workers as the builder who was supposed to supply the food neglected them and I needed to keep them on site.

Months went past and the building was supposed to be completed within seven months but I could tell that this builder was not going to complete the contract in the stated time. I relayed my concerns to my lawyer as I was now well ahead on the contracted payments. There were many meetings, some of which were theatrical including the builder shedding crocodile tears! Even my lawyer would say after the meeting that it was a good performance from the Balinese builder, but nothing was ever resolved in my favour. Hass never came to bat for me and always hung silently in the middle during any debate, meeting or confrontation.

In the end, surprisingly well past the contract completion date, my lawyer and the builder wanted to come to the villa to have a meeting. Now Hass and I had already moved in as my contract with the rented house was up and it couldn't be renewed and I didn't want to pay for another contract anyway. When we moved in, the doors and windows that were supposed to be completed at stage two still weren't in, there was no running water and I had to use this disgusting, outside, makeshift hole in the ground toilet that everyone used. I was appalled and felt really let down by them all. They arrived and my lawyer said the builder needed to borrow more money from me to pay for the building contract and other things. I spat the dummy! I had already paid that before the building was started! Now I knew that I was and had been ripped off for all these months. On top of that, they asked me to pay the electricity bills he was supposed to have paid for the past couple of months during the building process. Out of the five people sitting in the meeting, including Hass, not one person came to my aid or rescue. I was infuriated as I went upstairs to find money to pay for this electricity and a second building permit. I knew I was fighting a losing battle alone but it had gone past the point of no return.

Off they went. All I was left with was a signed document saying that he had borrowed this large sum of money from me. The only input from Hass was when he told me that if I didn't pay like he'd said on other occasions, then the building would stop and he asked what I would do then.

A bloody big help that was! He had made a suggestion, which at face value seemed okay, to have other contractors who he knew, come and do some of the other work which the builder had contracted and agreed to do but had not completed yet. He asked me to give a brother, who was not trustworthy, another chance to prove his integrity to the family by doing the painting of the place. He ripped me off by spending a large amount of money on the paint which had now been entrusted to him. As head of the family he should have done something about it but he did nothing. The other contractors Hass introduced to carry out the other work also ripped me off and again nothing was done about it.

I had no one I could personally turn to for help and advice. I was stuck. The contracted builder had taken off without finishing my villa and with all my money in his pocket. I was screwed over by them all and there was nothing I could do about it. I was far from the first person who'd had this done to them. Hundreds of Westerners have had the same thing happen to them and ended up losing everything and it is still happening to this day. No matter how much you try and stay ahead of the game and be on your toes, they get you. We then employed other workers, over a period of three years, to finally complete the villa, including rebuilding some of the shoddy workmanship that had been done under the contract.

I contacted my lawyers to see how I could get my money back from this embezzling bastard of a builder and they said I would have to take him to court and as I had so much evidence against him. I had receipts of the ongoing expenses, which amounted to hundreds of millions of rupiah, and video footage of the bad building which I would have to replace over time; I had a very strong case against him. They said they would prepare documents to submit to the judge for a court case. Then it all went silent. I waited and waited but heard nothing. My 57 text messages, 23 phone calls and several emails went unanswered by my lawyers. I went to their offices but could never find anyone. After many months, finally, one of the acting lawyers who was teamed up with my lawyer responded but only after we managed to find out where he was living. He said he would attend to it.

Time slipped by again until finally we had a meeting in a coffee shop. He said yes, we would apply to the judge for the case the following day, as we had sent threatening letters to the builder which he just ignored. Just before the meeting concluded he asked me, "How much are you prepared to offer the judge?'"

Insulted that he would even consider asking me this, I said, "Nothing. I will not bribe any judge as you know I have a strong case against him." He said, "Well, that is the only way you will win; being a westerner." I was appalled, even though I had been told by many Indonesian people that this is the way it is done here. Then I said, "Not that I am going to, but how much money are you talking about?" He replied, "You would be best to start offering him a minimum of ten million rupiah but if the builder also offers him money you would have to counter his offer with more and you could still lose." Words could not describe what I was thinking or feeling; I was so angry. Needless to say, that was the end of that.

Another lawyer said he could take it to court so I thought I would give it one last go. This time I set up a meeting with him, Hass, me and my close friend and her partner who were staying with us. He was an Australian QC barrister and thought this may have an influence on the lawyer not to screw with me. It seemed this lawyer was on board; he was another old friend of Hass. He told us that my first lawyer was not honest with me and was in the deal with my building contractor! Shock and horror to hear my suspicions confirmed!

He asked for money to do some government checks on the builder as I figured there was no point in taking him to court if, in fact, he had

nothing and no assets. Reluctantly I gave him the money he asked for. He said to us and my QC barrister friend that he would have results in four weeks. That time came and went and I heard nothing, at the end of the second month and also ignoring my requests by text and email, he answered by saying that he had no results and the money had gone. That was it, I was over it. No more. It was no longer going to disrupt my life. We are talking here of a total of four years of this hideous situation.

The beginning of 2009 was mainly a pleasant experience and nobody had intruded in our lives to create a problem or drama for us. We were writing and composing songs but my money had all been used up to the point that I could no longer produce copies to release the T'Sunami, Hearts That Weep CD. Each year that had gone past I'd tried and failed to have the finance to do what was my dream and help these poor victims and survivors of the dreadful natural disaster. Every anniversary of the disaster, I felt great disappointment.

Hass was singing at different venues, not only solo but with groups doing blues, rock and ballads. I was his number one fan, I absorbed every note, every lyric, it was my life, my medicine and it gave me an opportunity to chat with tourists. I still had no friends to go out for a coffee, lunch or even chat with. I missed that. However, it was not long before our lives were interrupted again. Mama had hurt her foot, which we didn't know until we called that day. She had done it the day before. On looking at it I said we needed to take her to the doctor but she would not go, playing it down as nothing. We urged her to take care of it because she could not afford to get it infected. We went to the chemist and bought medicine to clean the wound and bandage it up. On leaving, we told the extended family who were living there, especially his untrustworthy brother, that they must make sure the wound was bathed and the medicine applied twice a day.

A few days later we got a call saying, "You need to come look at Mama, she is sick, her foot is sick." Without saying a word to each other we went to check up on the situation. Mama was sitting on her bed and everyone else was buzzing around the place. Hass got the rundown from his brother and then we started taking the bandage off her foot.

Oh dear God, before completely taking off the rest of the gauze I could smell it. I was saying to Hass, “This is bad.” Sure enough, her foot and toes were all black.

I knew in my heart of hearts that this had already turned into gangrene, not that I had ever seen it physically. I felt shock and anger at the same time. Hass called his brother into the room straight away and got stuck into him. (Ah, so this man has a voice now!) I said, “Okay, now we must go to the hospital immediately, not a doctor.” I told him this was the worst possible situation for his mother to be in and said, “The news is very bad so prepare yourself. She has gangrene and is now going to need an operation and this didn’t need to happen.” ‘Why don’t these people get it?’ I thought. ‘Why doesn’t she understand?’ She was married to a westerner for many years.

As soon as she got into the emergency room at the modern hospital we had taken her to, they called in the specialist. I told Hass that his mama was probably going to have her foot amputated. Sure enough, no sooner had those words rolled off my tongue than the specialist said to Hass, “We must do tests now but she will need an operation within hours.”

I had to go home to check on the worker who was living at our villa. By the time I had travelled the 30 minutes to our little dirt road, my mobile rang and Hass said to me, “Mama must have an operation now, what do you think?” I knew this call would come and why, so I replied, “It is not up to me to make this decision, you and your brothers must decide. I will tell you, your mother needs this operation now; if she does not get it she will die.” I said I would go back to the hospital within the hour.

When I returned, Mama was already in the theatre being operated on. They were amputating half her foot and toes. We waited for her to come out of the theatre and not only got the report but there, in a bottle, were her toes and bits. ‘Oh yes,’ I thought, ‘is there anything that affects people here so that they will react?' I knew they all had emotional points where they did crazy things to each other to the point of killing.

We stayed the night and then I returned home to get Hass some fresh clothes. You see, in Indonesia, at any hospital, westernised or not, the majority of care of the patient is done by the family. The nurses administer medication but the family does the bathing and other things that in western society the nursing staff do. With this system, at any given time of the day and night, a bedside is overrun with family and or friends. They eat and sleep in the ward. There is little peace for the patient. Hass was always exceptionally good at attending to his mama as he loved her deeply; I think more than anyone else in the world. I travelled to and from the hospital but slept many nights on the floor there. It was my birthday on one of these nights but I had not said anything to Hass or his mother. As I slept he must have read my mobile messages because when I awoke he was embarrassed and told me that he was going to say happy birthday but had forgotten. No big drama as there were far more important things going on.

The hospital staff don't supply the medicines required for a patient who is in hospital, they hand you a prescription but you must go and source it from a pharmacy (an apotik) and then they will administer it. If they do bring any form of treatment you have to sign an invoice and pay for it then they treat you. We were running out to pharmacies night and day to get what was required during the two weeks Mama was in hospital. I knew the bill was going up and up for her stay and doctors examinations. I went quietly to the reception a couple of times to find out what the ever increasing bill was. I knew that nobody in the family had the money for this, so how was it going to be paid? The bill had to be paid before a patient was released.

On the day it was rumoured that she was being released, Hass had called one brother to come to the hospital. I was sitting there quietly thinking, this is crunch time. I made out like I was going outside for a cigarette and once again returned to reception. I had already, unbeknown to the family, made a payment of 10 million rupiah. While I was at the counter

I saw Hass out of the corner of my eye; he was on the stairs. He turned quickly and went back up the stairs. I was already paying the total remaining bill with my credit card. It was twenty million rupiah more. I went back upstairs and Hass and his brother said, "Can we talk to you? We need to ask you if you could help pay the hospital bill and we would all pay you back." This meant his other brothers would be contacted to contribute.

I held out the receipt and said, "I knew it would come down to this so I have paid the full amount." They said thank you and that they, the family of brothers, would give back the money.

You see, for five years I had been paying for everything, All our own bills plus everything for his mama to live, including weekly food, electricity, rental houses, phones, medical, schooling and any incidentals, so my money was rapidly disappearing, not forgetting the loss of money as a result of the builder who ripped us off. Many others were constantly borrowing from me through Hass as well. All the money I had left in Australia, invested for my future, was also gone. We are not talking dimes and pennies here.

Mama was released and she came back to live with us while she recovered. The contract on her rented house (roomah, as it is known there) had also come to an end and I did not want to have to pay such a large amount again to renew that place for others to come and squat at my expense. I was over it because no matter how I brought the subject up, nothing ever changed or was done about it. Hass attended his mama daily and really took over that side of things as well as his two little nieces who were also there. He would take the older one to school on the motorbike each morning and pick her up each afternoon.

People would come to visit his mama but it used to throw me completely as they would arrive in groups and just march into my house as though they owned it. It really annoyed me as I felt that not only was I ignored but I saw very little respect being shown to me by the other Muslim women. Now I had been to many Muslim roomahs in the years I'd been

living there and the behaviour was totally different when I was at their places. I did not appreciate being treated like a complete outsider and would just pull back in silence.

I'd got to know a lot of Muslim people during the Ramadan period each year as we often used to go to gatherings at a special Muslim organisation in the Renon, where Hass had a long standing family friendship going way back to his home country of Timor Leste.. Those ladies were always very nice to me and always greeted me warmly and affectionately. One of Hass's two nieces was a real handful and challenge and this is when I started to see the other side of Hass's character; a character that no friends of his ever knew about. It was awful when she did anything wrong.

His mother had told him one night, when he arrived home from singing, how the little one had taken my cigarettes and hid behind the gazebo smoking them. He questioned her first and found out that one of his brothers had allowed her to smoke his cigarettes. She was still a baby of three years old. I was shocked. Then he started in on her, yelling and yelling to the point that I went upstairs.

I heard her terrible screams and went down to find out what was happening. What I saw sent me into a rage. I said, "What the hell you are doing to her?" "Nothing," he said. I thought, 'I don't care if I break the rules of being silent,' because here was this little girl sitting in a fetal position against the wall. He was sticking cigarettes in her mouth! At that stage she had around five sticking out from her lips and he was adding more and lighting them, telling her to smoke them. I said, "Stop this now!" His reply was, "She has to learn." I looked at her arms and legs and asked, "What's this?" She had cigarette burns on her lower legs and arms and Mama was sitting on the bed laughing.

I yelled and said, "This is child abuse and sick! You cannot do this to her. If you were in a western country you would be arrested for child cruelty." I could not stand it any more. I picked her up and put her on the bed beside her grandmother and walked out of the room. We had an altercation when Hass came upstairs and I said, "Now we must find another roomah for your mother." She had been with us for three months and was well enough to have her own place again. I felt ill at what I had witnessed and having the other side of him revealed to me.

Over the coming weeks we found another place for Mama to move into and this one was only supposed to be for her, the girls and a helper so I made sure it no longer had extra bedrooms, thinking this would eliminate the problem of squatters, as I call them. Even though I knew the principle of Muslim society where you help others less well off or fortunate than yourself, I felt I had met the needs of many people here one way or another. I am a giver but if it does not come from my heart and I am intimidated into giving then I reach a stage where I dig my toes in. I was going broke at the expense of others and what they expected of me.

The place, to me, was shoddy so we bought paint and Hass and I spent a week painting the interior to make it nice for Mama. In the past I'd bought her a washing machine and fridge and furniture so that she would be comfortable in her old age. We moved her into her new place and kept a close eye on her as she had to learn to walk again and get her balance due to her missing toes. It was not long before things went back to the way they had been. Two of the sons had moved in with their wives. My plan of a place with only two bedrooms had made no difference, so I was back to paying out for everyone again. None of them worked or contributed anything.

Two other brothers and their families were coming from their island to Bali, for Idul Fitri (or Lebaran). This is the celebration that follows Ramadan, the month of fasting. Throughout Indonesia there is chaos as Muslim families travel to visit families and friends to be reacquainted, shake hands and ask forgiveness for any wrong doing, apologise and feast together. Many Muslims travel from island to island to celebrate the Muslim holiday. Some travel great distances for just a few days; others will spend two weeks with family.

A family meeting was called to discuss the hospital bill that I had paid. I thought Hass, being head of the family, would be the spokesperson but no, he took a back seat and the second eldest became the leader of the discussion. As he went around the room, stating each brother's position, he said that he could give 6 million rupiah, one other said he would give 1 million rupiah and the rest said they could give nothing, therefore the balance fell on Hass, which in theory meant me. They forgot that on top of that, the ongoing weekly visits to the specialist and medications should be included plus I had just paid out for another year of roomah rent. I was totally floored at the conclusion of this family meeting. Hass, in all the profound wisdom that he used to dish out to everyone, did not have one word to say. It seemed to me that he was not the head of the family, even though his brothers were intimidated and scared of him for some reason. After seeing how he treated his niece it didn't take much to work out. Other friends of his had told me that if you crossed him or got on the wrong side of him you would pay for it. He had even told me himself that some close friend of his said something about him one time and he found out about it.

After approaching this guy and asking him if he had said something, the guy said no, so he laid into him so badly that he ended up in hospital and then Hass went and paid his hospital bill!!!! But he also told me that he realised he had to change all that when he moved to Bali, in 1988, to attend university and that family friends from his home island had helped him to achieve this. I think Hass was now tiring of the family expecting us to do everything and pay for everything all the time. He blew a fuse one day when his mama rang up to say they were out of coffee and asked if we could buy some!

Chapter Five

Duped In Paradise

Chapter Five
Duped In Paradise

This is not in any brochure or magazine promoting life in Indonesia and Bali. I only found out after I was married that I could not leave the country like a free person. Being married to an Indonesian, whether male or female, if you want to go out of the country, even with your wife or husband accompanying you, you must have a letter of authority from your spouse giving you permission to leave. This must be given to the government and immigration authorities to grant you an exit from and entry into Indonesia. Westerners are seen as walking ATM machines; they think that because we obviously have more money than they do, we are rich. This is a fact; if you ask anyone living in Bali they will tell you the same thing. They don't realise and are not interested in the fact that the majority of us work bloody hard all our lives to have what we do, whatever the amount. A major focal point firmly in their minds these days is to marry a westerner and those who do are expected to take care of the family, no matter how far that extends and if we don't, then we can expect trouble.

When Hass came with me to Australia, what I found staggered me. On submitting our documents to the authorities, I was only given three weeks on my exit visa but Hass was given three months. When I left the country on my own I always had drama with customs when I came back in. They always greeted me by name before intensely looking over what I had brought back with me. When I came back in with Hass, we would always be waved through instantly with only a brief check of our passports. I remember having a debate with an expat neighbour later on and talking to him about us not having our freedom to go out or come in and he said he could come and go as he pleased and didn't need such a document. He then conferred with his Balinese wife. He was shocked when she confirmed what I was saying. He never knew he had to have her written permission.

Many Westerners also get confused thinking that Balinese people are not associated with Indonesians. Balinese people are in fact Indonesian but they are generally of Hindu religion unless they have managed to marry (which is rare) a person of another religion, then invariably they are quite often denounced by the family, but not in all cases. It is also uncommon for a westerner, or expat as we are called, to marry a Balinese. It happens more so in the case of Balinese men marrying a western woman than the other way round. This too, is misunderstood by many westerners as they think or assume that just because the Indonesian person is living in Bali, they must be Balinese. This is not the situation. Many thousands of Indonesians, both men and women, come from other parts of Indonesia. I would say that the majority are from Java and come to Bali to work as they are able to get more employment in the tourist industry and better pay than in their home areas. A lot of women from other islands and living in Bali seek out western men for husbands and many western men seek an Indonesian wife.

We continued with our life doing our own music in the daytime or when Hass was not singing. He had taught himself how to play the keyboard and had a natural talent for that also. He preferred to compose his own slant on established cover songs rather than rely on the midi music already installed on the new keyboard I had bought him. This was an original Yamaha 3000. I say that as many instruments in Indonesia, along with most products, are copies and they can be bought at a cheaper price than an original but of course break quickly too. Hass would often compose a piece of music and ask me to write some lyrics for it so I would sit there, get a feel for the music track and then it would just come to me. They were great times. I have written twenty or thirty original songs now, with a couple in particular still sitting and waiting to be recorded!

I had told Hass that the following year we could no longer afford to pay for Mama's roomah and that now it was the family's turn. I did not say this to be mean or nasty, I had told him that my finances were getting too low and we had to take care of ourselves. He understood what I was saying and agreed, even though people, not family, would still approach

him to borrow money. I'd started saying 'no' as I knew now that all the money I had loaned to people would never be seen again.

The time came around, at the end of 2009, when Mama's lease was due to expire. Hass discussed it with his brothers at different times and one brother had found a place at a reasonable price but it was not suitable for the younger niece who was very challenging with her strong, independent personality. Hass had found this little place up the road from us which Mama could even run a little business from, as she was an amazing baker and cook. Her cakes and donuts were to die for. This worried me purely because I wondered, if he found it, did that mean I would have to find the money to pay for it? One of the brothers living with Mama had seen it and given a negative report to Mama about it. He had little vision or positive attitude to most things. Anyway, he had completely turned Mama off it even though I said I would stretch to pay for it if the brothers put some money in too. It was a no go, which infuriated Hass as he had taken care of all his brothers for so many years, putting them before himself. It infuriated me and I said, "Well that is it, I am finished trying to help."

With that, Hass made a decision. He said, "Okay, the brothers always criticise me and they are jealous so now they can take care of Mama." He contacted his brother on another island and said, "Okay, you have always wanted to take care of Mama, now is your chance. She can come and live with you." The flight was arranged and they left within a couple of weeks. Mama and the girls stayed with us for a few days before going. I was worried as I didn't know if the brother knew how to take care of her diabetes properly, but once Hass makes a decision, that's it.

We said our goodbyes and Mama flew to Sulawesi and then on to their country area to live.

Hass still liked this little building up the road and said it would make a good business premises and brought me around to thinking about it. I said I would pay the lease, which was three years, but only on one condition; he had to be serious about it and really be responsible for his

business. He said he would. So out the door went another 52 million rupiah for him to have a daytime business; a Warung (small food café). I thought that with the hundreds of friends and people he knew in the music world, CB radio organisation he was in and old university mates alone, he could have a very successful business. He was a good cook and, like his Mama, made brilliant donuts. I never even used to eat them as I didn't like them but his used to melt in your mouth.

After months of preparing this place and forking out so much money I said, "Okay, no more, you must open for business now." In my younger days when I was working I had run coffee shops and done the full bit in hospitality so I knew we were ready. To try to increase the number of bums on chairs I suggested a little station for motorbike washing as it was right on the by-pass in a good location. It opened and a few people would come in. I had said to Hass, "Why don't you tell your CB radio friends about it? They could even have a gathering there on their outings." That fell on deaf ears. I started getting concerned. I would go up there some days and the worker we'd previously had finishing off the villa, who was living in and completing the Warung, would tell me Hass had gone to Denpasar. This would happen often.

He then came home one day with the brilliant idea of putting in some guy he had come across locally, on one of his days up there, just because he came from his childhood area. He'd gotten money off me, without me knowing, to get this guy an ID to live in Bali and the surrounding area. If I ever questioned or asked him about this stuff, I used to hit a brick wall. Things were quietly changing from how they used to be.

This guy was in there for a few months and at the end of the month I would go up there, check on stock and get the sales book and petty cash tin. There would be sales written down but very little money and nothing would balance. I would try to talk to Hass about this but he would shrug his shoulders. A couple of times when I pulled up there in the car, he was nowhere to be seen and this guy would be asleep on the chairs. I could take the money tin out and check everything and he would be asleep the whole time. I was tempted to take the money tin

one day and see what happened. This really pissed me off as Hass had gone back on his word about being responsible and to me it showed a lack of respect towards me again and what I had tried to do for him. He never stuck at anything for long, only singing.

After the months slipped by with no monetary return, I went up there one day to find that not only was he living there but two other people as well. One was a relation of Hass's from this same island. I knew him because he had been a worker on the villa in the early stages! I checked the stock. It was empty. Within a week, eight cartons of cigarettes were finished and the drinks were finished including all the bottles of beer. That was it. The money tin was empty and no one was around. I took the money tin and book home with me. When Hass returned home I said, "Okay, it's over. You are not serious about this business and this guy or someone is outright stealing from us. He has to go now, along with the others."

The only response I got was, "Well, what's the point? The government is widening the bypass and will wipe out the frontage of all the businesses." I thought, 'Well if there are going to be so many workers in the area they will need food, drink, petrol and a toilet.' It was useless; he had no interest in the business or making it into anything. It was closed and down the tube went a total of 56 million rupiah. The months it had been open meant high electricity, gas, petrol, food, drink and cigarette bills.

Hass had started withdrawing a little in communication but our relationship was still okay. We still spent leisure time playing music and he was encouraging me to sing and giving me confidence.

Within six months of Mama going to live with Hass's brother she had fallen seriously ill; suddenly from what we knew. We got a phone call to say she was in hospital. The doctor's report was grave, stating that her liver had gone. I said to Hass, "I am sorry but you need to prepare for the worst, your mama is going to go soon." We spoke to her on the phone from her hospital bed that night at around 11pm. At 2:30 in the

morning the call came through that she was gone. I was really upset at this news and felt deeply for Hass. There was no time to sit and chat, he had to ring his brothers in Bali, pack a bag and at 3.30am we were heading to a travel agent to get airline tickets for three of them. It seemed that I would not be going with them. We met the brothers at the airport, gave a sad hug and they left for Sulawesi. They had to travel many miles overland, after arriving at the airport, to get to the brothers place for the funeral ceremony to take place.

I felt empty and lost sitting at home alone. I still had no friends so there was no one to chat with for any comfort and I didn't know how long Hass would be gone. We spoke later that night and he said the service went well but he couldn't even cry. This seems to intrigue him but I knew he was in shock and utter grief even if he did not realise it. He returned about six days later with photos of the grave and of Mama laid out before they went to the cemetery. I just cried looking at those photos of her.

Beautiful, loyal Bo, now the grand old age of 15, was sick. His body weight was low and he struggled to go up the wide stairs we had especially designed for him so that he could get from one level to the other.

I tried to keep him downstairs but no matter what barrier I put up, he got around it to be by our side at night. He was failing even on them. When I took him for a walk he would get outside the gate and lie down. His spirit was amazing, like a pup, but he was ill and I knew that to be kind to him, I had to call the vet. She informed me that his blood was no longer getting to vital organs. I had spent two weeks knowing that when I called the vet, it would be his last day. Even now, just writing about him, I cry. I still miss him so much. The vet waited for me to give the word to put him to sleep. Both Hass and I were devastated. We cried in each other's arms and we cried alone. We had him placed in our garden. It was such a sad, sad day and it flowed into the weeks and months to follow.

By mid 2010 my finances were grim, to say the least. I thought about doing home stays as we had a guest room downstairs. We discussed it and thought it would be a way of getting extra income as I still wasn't allowed to work in Bali.

I set about organising a website through the family friend who had helped me buy my PC way back when my laptop was stolen. I had taken great shots of the property and wrote the promo out for it and he completed the website. I was getting enquiries from all over the world but most wanted to take over the whole villa for a period of time, even though I had clearly stated it was only suitable for a couple or a single person as we remained at the villa to take care of our guests. This was not working, so I had taken out a loan with another one of Hass's female business friends because the banks would not lend me money as I was not an Indonesian citizen. They wished they could help but Hass did not have a sustainable income to cover the loan. My Australian credit cards were maxed out and I was struggling to make the monthly payments on them now.

I did not like the conditions which were presented to me by the friend, where she not only held the original land certificate but also that she could come and take whatever she wanted at any time if she felt inclined to do so. I expressed my concerns to Hass and he just told me that if I want the money, this is the way it is. I was stuck between a rock and a hard place. I got scared off with the home stay as the government was cracking down and going around to villas that had been rented out without permits. I decided to quit the idea as I didn't need any more trouble with officials; I'd had my lot in the past. We had always talked about going back to Australia to give Hass the opportunity of a good singing career there, so we discussed selling the property and moving there.

I then changed the home stay website into a villa for sale.

The cruncher was coming and I knew it. Even with this loan, things were going from bad to worse as I now had to foot the repayments on

the loan as well. I had to sell some things to make ends meet and pay the growing debt. I started off by selling the furniture from the business which had originally been bought for Hass's mama. From there it became an ongoing process and I knew I had to sell the car next to try to slow the disaster of our financial situation. Later, I quietly realised that rather than preserving his musical status, if I had sold off all the expensive sound and extra musical equipment Hass had no interest in, instead of taking this loan, I could have saved myself a lot of grief.

Meanwhile, Hass was just doing his thing. He was now going out often during the day; to where, I don't know and on his return home he would laze around at his CB radio chatting with his buddies. If he wasn't singing he would sometimes go into the studio and play some music but this also became less frequent.

He was still singing three to four nights a week and I still enjoyed going with him. He had also started singing with his keyboard friend and a group doing country music. This was a new style for him, but like all the others, he just fitted in naturally. I love country music so really enjoyed listening to the band play at the restaurant each Saturday night. I got to know the owner who was a lovely little lady who had been married to an Italian man for many years.

I always looked forward to going there and having a chat with her and she was trying to help me find a buyer for the property. She came out with her staff one day to have a look at the villa and the sweetie had her chef make me a lovely meal to bring to us.

It was after her visit that she phoned to tell me that while they were having a look at the beach, which Hass decided to escort them down to, during a conversation he had with one of her people, he had told him that I was selling the villa and that 'he' had told me to go home (to Australia) because I couldn't work in Bali. This was a revelation to me. I was stunned and speechless. Say what???? What is this? I just replied to her, "Oh really! That is a lie, why would he say that?" She said, "Don't say anything to him as he might cause trouble." I agreed

and after the phone call went back over what she had said. I thought, why would she be afraid of him?

Wow! This put a whole new perspective in front of me and I wondered what he was up to. We were meant to be going back to Australia together. I was glad she had told me this as I now had to observe what was going on around me more closely and to be careful. What other lies had been told? There was obviously something afoot that I was totally unaware of.

Chapter Six

Warning Bells Were Ringing

Chapter Six
Warning Bells Were Ringing

He was changing, his mood swings were becoming more obvious to me and communications were shutting down to suit his needs.

I had to sell the car. The time had come. This was a big decision for me to make as I realised that once the car was gone, if Hass was out on his motorbike, I had no transport at all. It was my mental source of independence, even though it was rare for me to go out alone. Being a Muslim wife, you are not meant to go out alone, unless your husband tells you to. Sometimes I went to his mama's or did some shopping. I told Hass that we had to do this but it was met with very little comment. I placed an advert in the local western free paper, at a reasonable price to get a quick sale. I had many responses straight away and in fact, I sold it to the first caller. It was gone.

I would now need to go on the back of the motorbike if I was going anywhere, including gigs to listen to Hass sing. I then noticed an even bigger change in Hass's behaviour. I remember within about a month of selling the car, getting on the back of the bike to go with him to a gig. It was raining.

He was really angry as he started up the motorbike and I couldn't work out why. My inner voice said to me out of the blue, 'Why is he so angry about going out in the rain? I'm not, and if anyone should be, it should be me.' I thought about it all evening while he was singing and it was like a light switching on. 'Oh, I get it now,' since being with me and having all the luxuries he was seen as having status. His friends would even joke with him about it in front of me and laugh, including him. I used to ask what was so funny, but not get an answer. Ah! I had embarrassed him in front of everyone by selling the car because I had, in all innocence, diminished his status. I knew I was in trouble.

I paid off my credit cards in Australia and more off the local loan and bought some food. That only lasted for so long and I had to pull back the money I had paid on my credit card to pay the loan. I knew I had to keep selling stuff as there was no money to pay the electricity bill.

Meanwhile, I noticed he had stopped coming to join me during the breaks on a Saturday night and stayed out the back. He was spending a lot of time texting on his mobile. The next Saturday night I was actually in the toilet, which backed onto the men's loo, and I heard him sweet talking on his phone to someone. Now he knew hundreds of women and it was pointless being jealous of anyone as he performed at different times with stunning women and ladies. I passed it off, thinking it was just another one of his friends although it was strange to go to the loo to make the call away from the other band members.

He had become 'very busy' during the day organising a CB radio reunion which was still months away and I wondered what was going to take that long to organise; it was only a one day event.

We would always pick up food on the way home from a venue if they did not supply Hass with a meal during the break. He did not eat during an evening performance; generally afterwards. I always ate with him so I also waited to eat and it had been our habit for years. We always ate together. Sometimes coming home from this venue, he would ride straight past the shop even if I said we needed to stop and get food. Once home he would say he forgot to get food and would go back. He would drop me off and head back down the highway. I could have made something at home but he would refuse.

He would now turn on his CB radio as soon as we got home, eat the food and continue chatting on the CB. I would either watch TV or maybe go on the computer for a while. He would giggle and chat away to the men and women of the organisation then fall asleep on the couch, often with the CB in his hand. One night I decided to do what I had never done before and check his mobile. There were all these text messages from a woman. I didn't understand what they were saying so copied them

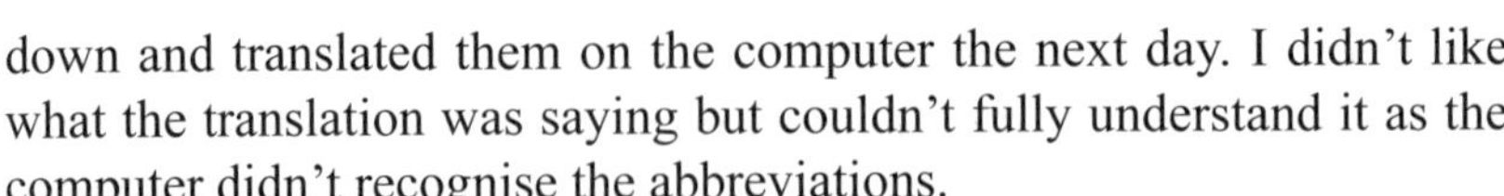

down and translated them on the computer the next day. I didn't like what the translation was saying but couldn't fully understand it as the computer didn't recognise the abbreviations.

The next time I was in town I went to the main book store and asked if they had a book on Indonesian abbreviations. The lovely assistant said they didn't and asked if I wanted her to translate something for me. You see, the pure translation on the internet is not the same as the spoken interpretation in Indonesia and to add to the confusion there are over 2,000 different dialects. She came back quite embarrassed and gave it to me in its entirety. I was as shocked as she was. Just to check this again, so I would know for sure, I did have two Indonesian friends who were honest and open with me so I sent the messages to them for interpretation. I immediately got a reply back from one of them asking where I got this bad language from; so I told her. I could tell they were equally as shocked as me.

It said, (excuse the bluntness of this) I have cleaned my fanny and am waiting for you; ring me when you finish singing. Can you make yourself clean to come to me?

Now I knew my suspicions and intuition were correct all along. I was devastated.

You know exactly what you would do if you were in your own country, but I wasn't!!

I never said anything, thinking that maybe he would get over it and stop. Another reason for my shock was that only a few months before he was still writing on my Facebook wall saying, 'I love you honey forever and ever,' for the entire world to see.

The phone calls started next. She would ring him every morning around nine and I would wake to hear him in whispered conversation with her that would last for an hour or so, making out he was talking to some old friend. My heart was being torn apart piece by piece each day. There had been a few enquiries about the property via email but nothing serious.

I was selling my belongings bit by bit and strategically on the bigger items to raise as much money as I could to not only pay the loans but meet the electricity and other bills as well.

The following Saturday night I got ready to go with Hass and was shutting the door as he walked past me to go to the garage for the motorbike. As he walked past me he said aggressively, "You stay home." I said, "Pardon?"' "You stay home." I was struck dumb for a moment and as I walked towards the gate he ignored me, so I said, "I am meant to see Millie tonight about the property. I need to come." He left me standing there. I was seething.

A couple of times I went to his other venues in Kuta but found he would ignore me all evening. As this was fast becoming the only time that I got out of the villa I tried to silently stand my ground without causing any waves.

One evening, after he got home from singing, I asked him, "Would you please take me into town tomorrow so that I can get my mobile fixed?" He knew it had been playing up. I said, "You can just drop me off and go and do what you have to and we can meet up when you are finished. I will just have a walk around." (He was still organising the reunion with this delegated woman.)

Out of nowhere, in a split second he had upended our large, glass-topped coffee table sending coffee cups and all flying everywhere. He got up and slapped me hard across my face and said, "I have plans." I muttered stunned, "All you have to do is drop me off, you don't need to stay with me, you can do what you want." I got up and went into the glass partitioned office. He followed me in, kicking the plastic set of draws and yelling at me, "What, you think I go f.........g or something?" I said, "I never accused you of anything, they are your words." He kept on, "I can have any woman I want to f.........k, I can have young, old, fat, skinny; you want I do that??"

I stood there in a complete state of numbness. He then realised that he had cut his toe open from kicking the draws and went limping off to the bathroom to get ointment and cotton balls and came back cursing that his foot was cut. Later he said sorry for hitting me but I should not disturb his mind, that he can only concentrate on one thing at a time. I thought, 'What a load of bullshit.'

The next morning he dropped me off in town and took off. The plan was that he would contact me when he was ready. My top lip was bruised, which I covered with makeup. Now that he had shown his guilty conscience to me by his outburst over nothing at all, I knew my problem was far worse than I had imagined it to be. Who was this woman?

As the day drew on and I had not heard anything I decided I would go to this woman's place, where he had been organising the reunion from. She was very surprised to see me at her door and as I looked inside I saw the CB radio mates that were there. There seemed to be some kind of panic, not only in her eyes but in the body language of the others. They said my husband had gone home but I could come in. I said, "It's okay, I will go." I thought, 'There is no way he has gone home without me.' I walked back down her long laneway to the main street and towards the corner. I had called Hass on his mobile and told him where I was.

He told me to wait there and that he'd be there to pick me up. Meanwhile, the woman came on her motorbike from the house I had just left, in what seemed like a state of panic. She had my motorbike helmet in her hand. How interesting I thought, as I now knew that she was also lying to me about his whereabouts. She was looking in every direction for him to come. You see, I think she was expecting him to come down the road with his woman on the back of the bike. Her behaviour was so extreme for someone who was just going to wait with me till he turned up. I told her she could go home but she ignored me and insisted on waiting with me.

'Oh the games people play,' I thought to myself. He turned up about five minutes later and off we went. Hass was singing that night and I

decided I was not going to go with him; there was way too much tension in the air and I already had a bruised upper lip from the evening before.

A week later I got ready to go with him again on the Saturday night. He had watched me get ready and we got outside the door. I went to unlock the padlock on the gate and then went back to lock the house.

As I did this he started his motorbike and drove out the gate. I thought he was just going to wait out there like normal while I closed the gates but no, he kept going. I ran out of the gate and yelled out but he kept going. The local farmer saw this and yelled after him too. I felt humiliated standing there all dressed up but more so because I knew this would spread around the local village. I was furious all night. When he came home he had no food with him and I had not eaten since the day before. There was nothing in the house because there was no money. The little wage that he got at one place he sang at was only paid once a month or every five weeks. At the nightly gigs he now only gave me half of what he was paid. Before all this started he had always brought it all home. I was lucky to see 50,000 rupiah ($10) from a nights pay,

I never spoke to him when he came home and he just got straight onto his CB radio.

Hass would go out early in the mornings now or be on the phone, to guess who? It was sickening. I decided there and then that it would be the last time I would attempt to go with him for a while in order to watch him sing. I couldn't stand being humiliated again, at least for a while. Time passed and I was still selling what I could, when I could but I was placing an advert in the paper every week with something for sale. I sold off all the extra things first, table and chairs, fridge, washing machine, some large tool items like bench saws and stuff I had brought with me from Australia. As you know, when you sell anything, no matter how good the condition is, you lose money on it. To top it off, even westerners coming to buy stuff had gone into Indonesian price negotiation mode so I was losing huge amounts of money but I did all I could do to try and save the situation.

At night when I was there alone I would sometimes turn on the CB radio as they were real gossipers. I would hear things about Hass and his woman and even though this woman was a Muslim she obviously had no morals about committing adultery.

One night he was singing in Kuta and told me the hours had changed but he had embellished the hours as I soon learned. I heard him whispering on the CB radio and he was saying that he was in the Renon area and there was lots of giggling then her name was mentioned and she too came on the CB with him talking briefly to the responding party. He was supposed to finish singing at 11pm but it was already that time as I checked my watch. He returned home at 2am saying that after singing he had to take a microphone to a venue down the road and then got talking to his muso friends there. Oh really? I responded with, "That's nice," but I thought, 'You lying shit.' He was, in actual fact, just fifteen minutes down the road. All this nonsense went on for months but he must have told his CB radio mates to be careful if I listened in, because one night I had not had the gate padlocked and he quietly snuck into the house without me knowing. I didn't even hear his motorbike come home. I freaked out when I saw him coming up the stairs and tried to turn off the CB but it was too late.

After that, there were many times when I would hear gossip about Hass and his woman but then someone would chip in with "hati hati," meaning "be careful" or they would make funny sounds and then the person would laugh and change what they were saying.

I checked his phone at different times and noticed he now had code names for her listed in his contacts, but all had the same number. Oh, did he think I was that stupid? He started turning his phone off when he went to sleep but little did he know, and I had never used it before, that about a year before that I had watched him for no particular reason, putting in his password to open his phone. A few times I used it when he was asleep to try and find out the situation. I would go downstairs with it, really nervously, to where I knew our phones got no signal as I didn't want any messages to come in when I had it open. I would write

down the messages and translate them when I was safely on my own.

You may be thinking what a terrible person I am to do that and that's okay with me, but I was living in a strange country that I could not just walk out of, sorry, fly out of and there was no one to protect me and I had no friends there I could go to or talk with. It seemed as if Hass had all this backup from his buddies, many of whom were of his religion, and it horrified me that they encouraged this love affair. I think they got off on it as entertainment as the majority of them were either middle aged or heading in that direction. Men and women alike were all part of this, even though they knew me.

I was scared; what would become of me? What would become of me when the property sold? Was he playing with her until it was sold and then still planning on going to Australia or did he have some other plan for me?

Had I been back in Australia I would have tackled it head on but I could not do this in Indonesia, especially now that I had been attacked by him once already. I had to remain cool and quiet. Weather the storm, so to speak. I knew that Indonesian women who had found out their husbands were cheating on them either sucked it up because they had children or the brave women would get hold of the woman in question and give it to them. Adulterers can be prosecuted in Indonesia if they are found together. In places like Ache, if a couple commits adultery and get caught, they are still, to this day, put in the street, stripped naked and stoned by the village. This practice still happens and you can read about it in the papers.

I had spoken to several women, both Balinese and Indonesian, who spoke English and they told me their awful stories of their husbands repeatedly betraying them.

They said they could not leave because if they did they would lose their children to him and his family, so they just focused on raising the children. The other reason they could not leave was because their own

families would also abandon them. These are terrible circumstances for women, having to live their lives like this. One friend, Ketut, told me that she had caught her husband not only with her young niece, but also another woman and could not do anything. A few of them knew their husbands had two or three illegal wives and children. Those poor children could not go to school because the woman was not legally married and could not get a certificate as proof of a legal marriage.

It continued. I would go to wash his clothes when he came home from singing and I found his shirts to be drenched with sweat. Now I knew his clothing well and even after singing on a New Years Eve his clothes were never wet from collar, to sleeves, back and front. I also found make up on T-shirts; powder and lipstick; it was all so obvious.

The reunion event was coming up and he was seldom at home now, day or night, and at night he was coming home between 2am and 4am so those nights I went hungry many times. Ramadan came and I was left, not only to open on my own in the evening, but he would turn up just before dawn when I would get to eat something, usually a little bit of rice and a small piece of chicken. I would wait to pray with him but he would make out that he was asleep so I would end up doing sholat by myself. This was very upsetting for me. I used to cry a lot while trying to pray. He would wait till I went to bed then get up just before dawn and do his sholat. I wondered what others of his faith would think if they knew what he was doing to me. He was told by the Imam who married us that he must not only take good care of me and keep me from all harm, but teach me Islam. He told me I could learn it from books. Up until this time he had always included me in everything.

It came to the final morning when Ramadan ended; it was at dawn each year that everyone went into the parks for mass prayer and the celebration of the end of fasting. I was ready and waiting to go with him. He left me at home. I cried and cried when he left. He sent me a standard text message some time later, after the breaking of Ramadan. I gave him some money to buy cookies as the family always came to visit in the morning, usually for the day. They arrived home before he did,

which was around 10am. I could not tell them where he was as I didn't know, even though I had my suspicions.

He used the excuse that he rode around for hours looking for a place to buy cookies!!! I checked his phone later that night and as soon as he finished praying he had sent her a message saying, "Honey, are you awake?" in Indonesian of course but I did understand the Indonesian. I understood more than I could speak for some reason. Once fasting had finished for the month, I spoke about us making love. I was told, "You are still fasting!"

The night before the reunion, he was out for hours preparing it. I'm not sure how much you can prepare in the dark as this was to be at a beach location where there was a stage area. I rang him to see how long he was going to be and he said he was just walking to his motorbike and that is where he made the slip. He actually called it the name of a large karaoke place and quickly covered his mistake and said the beach location which had a similar name. We went there the next morning. I was nervous as I knew somewhere in amongst the two hundred odd people, she was there. I also had to sing my song, Mama's Heart, at the venue. It was a song that I had written for my own children but one that any mother could relate to. It was a blues music composition that Hass had composed.

On arrival he said, "You sit over there," meaning under the huge marquee where there was a woman sitting in the front row. Her face was not familiar to me and as many came from other places for the event I thought she was one of them. I knew the local people. I sat down and she indicated for me to sit beside her. I sat and introduced myself by saying my name and that I was Hass's wife. She replied, "I know who you are."

'Oh God, has my worst nightmare just happened?' I thought to myself. "Sorry, what is your name?" I asked. She said, "E..." Oh my God, how could he do this to me? This was her!!!! And he told me to sit next to her while he was going to be on stage most of the day playing the keyboard

and looking down on us both. How sick is he, and she? What is wrong with him? I had heard the CB mates on air during the week laughing about this upcoming event, saying how funny it was going to be with photos and the general day. Now I knew why, I was a laughing stock in front of them all.

I made the excuse that I needed to go to the toilet. I could no longer sit beside her and take this. On my return I sat a couple of seats away from her so it wouldn't be too obvious that I knew what the hell was going on here. She had made up a plate of food from the dish in front of us and went to hand it to me. I wanted to throw it in her face but politely refused it saying, "No thanks, I have to sing later." I waited a few minutes then I picked up the plate and said to her, "Actually I must take this to my husband, he has not eaten yet," and I walked away after adding a little more to the plate.

Later in the afternoon Hass walked towards me. I watched his eyes and he kept them directly on me but his body was not taking its usual casual stroll. I would call it 'an uncomfortable body stance.' He told me I would be singing after the next person and then returned to the stage.

I was as nervous as hell but got encouragement from his assistant organiser. I was surprised she was so excited for me to sing and was quite vocal about it. She was also doing her own cover up which she thought I was oblivious to. I played along.

At the end of the first line, where the song hits a minor cord, there was huge applause from everyone that I was not expecting. This gave me confidence in their enjoyment, (maybe I was kidding myself maybe this was also just part of the game). I finished my song and received another huge round of applause. I didn't go back to sit near the other woman, I stayed at the side of the stage and felt relieved to be away from her. Towards the end of the program Hass did some dancing to dangdut music which is sexy and spicy and when women do it, it is very sensual. He can really dance and he was showing off. 'She' was sitting over there smiling with her body moving and trying to hold and hide her giggles.

She glanced over at me, smiling, and I just looked blankly back at her.

They had started packing up and I was trying to help. A couple of us tried to pull paper from this board it was stuck on, then someone asked who did this and a voice from behind me said, 'Oh, that was Hass and ECH last night.' Ah, there you have it, other suspicions confirmed. My intuition was working just fine so I must continue to pay attention and not go against it to cover the truth of what I know. The next thing, I saw madam coming towards me, she passed right by Hass but did not look in his direction or he in hers. I thought, 'Jeez, these two are so controlled and clever.' The next thing I hear from her is, "Bye, I am going home." I thought, 'I don't give a shit, good,' but muttered "Okay."

I was glad that day was over and was looking forward to just going home with Hass as it was his birthday the next day and I was hoping his present would fit him. He had finished the packing up with everyone and they were getting into their cars. His female organiser friend hadn't got in the car with friends that would be going right past her place and she came over to us and saying she had no transport. I asked, "Why don't you go with your mates?" but she gave some weak excuse. I said, "Let's call a cab for you and I will pay for it," as she only lived a few blocks away from the venue. It was around 8.30pm.

She refused my suggestion then Hass said he'd take me home and come back for her. I thought this was ridiculous as we lived 25 kilometres away and that was just one way. Again I said, "Well that is crazy, let us just get her a taxi." My suggestion was overridden and he told her to wait there, he'd be back in fifteen minutes; more like half an hour! He came inside, changed his T-shirt and went back out. He returned home at 3am.

He said he'd dropped her off then went on to a friend's place for a wind down party and fell asleep. He had red marks all over his back like a coin had been used to scrape his back rib cage area, from the back of the shoulders all the way down towards his buttocks. It is the traditional way, they believe, of bringing up wind from the stomach. It seems to

work to some degree. I remarked on this and he said that the guy had done it. Now that is feasible but the truth will be revealed a little later.

Everything he had ever said to me about never crossing the line, even espousing all his wisdom to people old and young and including one of my daughters on her visit, that he would never have anyone and would never cross the line was just a load of crap. The next morning he woke up and said he was going to see some band friends and to a meeting then he would be home. I had asked him to let me know when he was on his way home and not to forget that we were going to one of our favourite restaurants to celebrate his birthday. He said he would let me know.

While waiting for him to arrive home I got prettied up and dressed ready to go. 5pm came but no phone call. I tried to call him but his phone was switched off. It was the same at 6 and 7pm. My stomach was starting to sink. I tried to reach him again and got nothing and no response to my texts either. The night passed on. I sat there waiting. Eventually I thought I would just turn on the CB and see if I could hear anything. Sure enough, there was talk about them, so I recorded what was being said.

He was at some disco karaoke place with three women, one of whom I think you can guess. Here I am, sitting all dressed up with his gift, a nice leather jacket all beautifully boxed up and again I feel like a fool. I cried, I raged and then fell into depression, wondering what to do. He finally walked in at midnight and said, "Sorry, I fell asleep at the band friends place." I asked, "Which band friends place was that?" "Oh, people you don't know." He said, "Sorry, I make mistake to fall asleep and my phone had empty battery." The words fell out of my mouth, "Yes you make big mistake." I scrambled around to make a little food to eat.

He was busy the following two weeks at the printers, putting the photos together of the reunion and collating the business side of the reunion for a final meeting which was coming up. Many of the applications, to hold this day in a public place, had to have signatures on them. Now

Hass had shown me on several occasions just how well he could forge anyone's signature, including mine!

After watching and observing him over the past few months, I realised that if he ever wanted to, he could doctor any paper he required. This was a worry, even though I never thought he would do it with me. I stored that in my memory banks all the same. He started coming home later and later in the evenings so I started going with him to one of his venues again. This time though, I had another motive for tagging along.

I had been concerned about the way the loan was set up with his friend and even though I was grateful for her help, the fact that she was holding my original land certificate and her other option of being able to take anything if she felt like it, never left my mind and stressed me constantly. I told my daughter about this and that I was now feeling very uneasy for some reason and so she and her husband took out a loan in Australia and sent me the money that I owed so that I could pay the woman out and get my certificate back.

I thought it wise not to tell Hass about this because from the time I had met him until now, I had been a totally open and honest book about my life, but it was biting me in the bum. The only way I could withdraw the money was in stages and small amounts through the ATM. I figured that if I went with him when he was singing, I could go and withdraw money a couple of times a week until I had enough. This was going to take me about three weeks to complete because it was a large amount of money.

The heavens must have been with me as it all went according to plan. The week before it was all done he got a gig filling in for a night of singing and although it was a last minute situation, I made damn sure I went with him. I could tell he didn't like it much but by now I didn't care. While he was singing I went to an ATM which I had spotted on the way in, at the front of the venue. Perfect. I went for my stroll. During the break he actually sat with me, which he hadn't done for ages, and I thought, 'Hello what's up? This is a nice change,' and just accepted it at

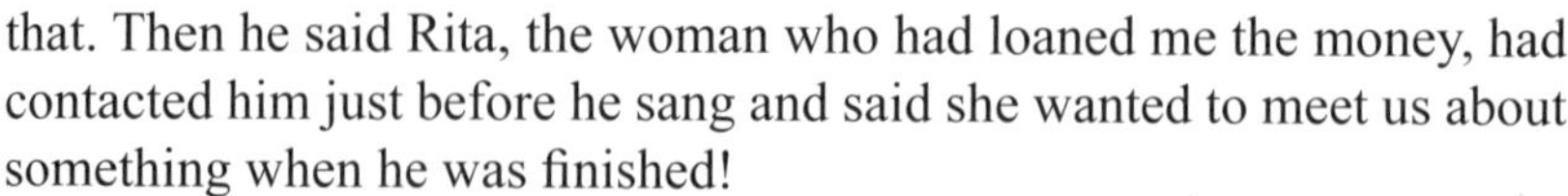

that. Then he said Rita, the woman who had loaned me the money, had contacted him just before he sang and said she wanted to meet us about something when he was finished!

"Okay, we can do that can't we?" Meanwhile, straight away my intuition had kicked in. Then he throws a second curve ball at me, "Oh and also Ning," the woman he organised the reunion with, "she has a problem and needs some money and asked if I (meaning him) would help her," and he gave me the story.

Trying to keep my composure, I said, "Well, you know our situation, we don't have money to lend anyone, I only have the money I have saved to pay the electricity bill, but we can go there after we see the other person and talk in between." I was ready. I tried to give an outward appearance of calm but I was almost vomiting from nerves.

While he was singing I quickly got busy and translated what I was going to say to his friend as I had already guessed what this meeting was about. I didn't want him translating to her what I had to say as I would not fully understand it, especially if he used their homeland dialect. She was there with a guy who I had met before, a young man, very sure of himself and which touched on arrogance. We sat down and the small talk began. I thought, let's just cut to the chase as this young man sat opposite me staring me out. I wasn't going to let him play his silly games, so blocked his eyes from my face with my hand and turned side on towards my husband and the woman. Many people are very good at hypnotising you at any time!

I broke the small talk and said, "What is it Rita wanted to meet about?" Hass then relayed to me just what I had surmised were her reasons for the meeting. She wanted to use the land certificate for some job tender she had an interest in. With that, I interrupted and said my piece. "I am very sorry but next week you will be paid out in full on the loan as I need the land certificate for potential buyers who are coming." For once my Indonesian was understood. They sat there stunned. She asked Hass how I could pay it back and where the money was coming from.

I found this out later when talking to him. Of course he could not give her any answer as he didn't know. The meeting was over so we went to the next one.

It was all friendly and nice and we sat on the floor doing the lead up to what she wanted. She then pulls out this receipt, like from a loan shark, where she had put all her jewellery to get money some time before. Many people had to do this in Indonesia when they needed cash. The bottom line was that she needed 10 million rpt straight away. I sighed deeply, like many times before, as I had told him the previous year that he mustn't even tell me when people ask to borrow money because we can't help anyone any more. I hated saying 'no' to people because yes, we did technically have more than them; we had a villa but zero cash flow. They believed that no matter what you told them you must have money just because of this alone. The money I had coming was all going to the woman who loaned us the money so I could pay her out; there was no extra cash left over.

I looked at the three phones she had sitting around and asked, "Why you don't sell one or two of your mobiles?" No, she couldn't do that for some reason. I tried to think of other ways she could get the money together but then Hass would chip in and say, 'These were heavy mafia type dudes that had been to her house asking for the money.' In the end I said, "Look, all we can loan you, I am sorry, is 1 million rupiah and that is our electricity money but we have to pay the electricity in two weeks time." "Oh yes, thank you, I will give it back to you." Mmmm!!!

After that, she complained about her neck and shoulders being so sore, so I said turn around I will give you a massage.

I pulled back her top slightly and lo and behold there before my eyes were the red coin markings completely down her back ribs, just like Hass's back. Immediately I lifted my hands and looked at him. He looked down towards the ground and then she started saying, "Oh, Hass is very good to do …" (gasp!) I saw him glare at her. I had just been jabbed with a knife, or it felt like that.

I already knew something had been going on with her at the same time

as the other woman because on other occasions he gave the game away, and so had she. He was very familiar with her bedroom; breezing in and out of it and he knew exactly where stuff was when she asked him to get things. She was a middle aged widow. The other one, I don't know about except that she has what seems to be four children in their teens to early twenties. I wondered how many of them he was screwing. My God…and did they know about each other? I know that the one who had just borrowed money from me knew about madam and used to cover for him.

What he has never realised was that while he never ever uttered a word about her to me, she had no trouble broadcasting their relationship over the CB radio for anyone to hear and she used to gossip about them all the time. They also had no morality because they would parade around the town for anyone to see them together. I got various reports sent to me from some of his so called friends telling me he was out with this woman. He was breaking the laws of marriage according to the holy Quran and he/they knew it. He had even been seen being spoon-fed by her and their feely touchy romance was in public view.

If a Muslim man has an interest in another woman and wants to be with her, he must have written permission from his first wife and especially if he wishes to marry her. He cannot marry her without this. It is a clear and stated fact of the marriage rule book given out when you get married. I don't know what lies he had obviously told her, as he was or had become a compulsive liar, believing his own lies completely. If he had told her we were divorced then she had been totally lied to and deceived. We were not. He had never spoken a word about her or mentioned her name to me and he sure as hell had not even uttered the word divorce to me, ever. I had never signed any document pertaining to this.

I recalled that one of the workers at the house bravely spoke up and said to me one day, when my husband was out, "Ibu, tida (no) let them take all kamu (you) berapa, Ibu (mother, woman,) berapa (money) habis (finished) kamu, (you) be garbage!!!!." Wow! That blew me away

coming from him. His past words rang out of nowhere in my head. He has since passed on but I will always remember that powerful statement he made, as I had heard similar words from other Indonesian people also.

Many, many western people have ended up in this position after finding love and trusting the people in Bali and other parts of Indonesia. There are constant stories of this happening, mainly to men. I knew of a beautiful lady from Sweden that this had happened to and she had devoted herself to helping young ones in poverty while married to a Balinese man. She was lucky to get out with her children and their suitcases and go back to her homeland.

Another kind-hearted Australian lady, whose name I won't mention to protect her privacy, also married an Indonesian and lost her villa. On returning from a holiday back home she found her husband had moved his other wife and children in; he had not told her about them but had moved them into the villa she had built and told her to get out, she had no rights there. She returned home to Australia with nothing.

One day I met another one called Faye. She had just arrived in Bali that day, after escaping back to Australia from her Indonesian husband who had brutally abused her. She was terrified to be back and was so anxious, even while just standing there talking in the street. I really felt for her. The only reason she had snuck back in was to try and sell her block of land which she had had to ignore for the past six years. She was leaving the following afternoon as she felt so unsafe. She has not been back since then and her land still sits with ever-growing weeds while she tries to get it sold.

There are hundreds of stories, all true, within the western community; there are countless similar situations, as well as people losing the money they invested in building villas. Many have returned to their home countries, shattered, with nothing left but broken dreams. Many have fallen ill, believing that black magic has been put on them; a subject very much alive there but spoken softly of or not at all. It is a

strong belief not only of Balinese Indonesians but the general populous of Indonesian people.

Many local people fall ill from what they believe to be black magic because of something they have done in the past, which they regret, or a family member, either currently living or back in the generations somewhere. Many never recover and pass away. They don't normally seek medical attention from modern society and rely on the village priest or Imam to pray for them or a member of the community will give them jamu (local herbal medicine) which goes back in history.

There are also many expats who have suddenly fallen ill and those who believe or have allowed their minds to admit to black magic seem to take a long time to recover.

There are many beliefs that the Indonesian people have which is full of supernatural forces such as ghosts and spirits, good and evil, which can disturb your life. They are very afraid of this, even though they make many ghostly TV series of people turning into huge snakes or the walking dead. The whole family watches these programs, including little children from the age that they can walk and talk.

This is one of the many reasons that they have their special ceremonies once a year; to cast out evil spirits and visitors of the spirit kind from their compounds and homes in Bali. It is the Balinese ceremony called Nyepi, the most important part of the saka calendar. The night before the silence there is a spectacular competition with all the villages making larger than life statues representing devilish things. They are paraded through the streets in the evening with the noise and energy levels of the local people involved in carrying the statues reaching a crescendo before the statues are burnt. Many are now sold after the event even though they are meant to be burnt to get rid of the evil spirits.

Every single person must abide by the 24 hours of total silence, with no lights on; you cannot go out into the streets. There are special Balinese patrols that make sure nobody is abusing this stillness throughout Bali.

All aircraft are grounded and no craft may fly in during this period. Tourists may quietly walk around their resort but may not go out of the grounds onto the beach or street. Resorts organise special meal times and very low light for dining. All entertainment ceases during this period.

There are many expats who are trying to achieve the near impossible goal of controlling the garbage in Bali, which has reached epic proportions. They are doing a wonderful job at promoting a clean and green Bali but it will take a very long time for education to filter through to all age groups. The huge increase in the tourism trade, which is blowing out, is also contributing to this problem. There are great expats also involved and committed to helping the street kids and children in orphanages, which is fantastic. You are such amazing people.

I had cause one evening while Hass was singing, to go and visit the lovely lady doctor as she was only a couple of buildings away from where he sang. She treats many western people who reside in Bali and she has a high profile in the community. She is a very good doctor and lady and is also part of the CB network. I was sick but had put off going to anyone due to lack of finances. While she was examining me I broke down. I was in a very depressed state because of what had been happening. She, of course, wanted to know why I was so upset, so I revealed what I knew. She was very concerned for me and was most disapproving of what was happening to me and what Hass was doing. I appreciated that she had genuine empathy towards me. She also told me that there was no way that organising the reunion should take months of consistently long hours at night, as it was just a social event.

She gave me some suggestions and also wanted me to have some x-rays the following week to check if I had recovered from my sickness. Fortunately the medicines she prescribed had me well by week's end.

Chapter Seven

Beaten Into Submission

Chapter Seven
Beaten Into Submission

*"But for my faith in God,
I should have been a raving maniac."*

Mahatma Gandhi

We had been invited late in October, 2010, to fly to another island to attend a very large family wedding. We had no money to pay for airline flights but had been told that was all taken care of. I was happy to be going out of Bali as a couple of weeks before I had found hidden, in a special performance jacket Hass seldom wore, a brand new ladies watch. My heart sank as we did not even have food to eat unless he performed. In the other pocket I found another watch, it too looked new. I then started going through his clothes that were hanging up and found hidden money. Where did that come from? I took photos of it all. I showed them to someone, a friend who had come to the house to do something, the next day.

Two nights before going I was alone at home as Hass was singing. Looking at the beautiful wedding photos that were done in a studio in Australia during our honeymoon there were a few gorgeous photos of us which I wanted to add to my special memories album on Facebook. When we brought the album home Hass had said that we must keep it to ourselves and not show Mama and he asked me to agree to this, which I did. However, we had shown family and friends in Australia and everyone thought the photos were beautiful.

They were not 'bad' photos or anything like that; they were very romantic, moody and fun shots and we had a great time shooting them. I had a bra top on and jeans and he had his shirt off. He had put shots

of himself with no shirt on in his Facebook photos and with Mama having passed on did not see a problem with it. My albums were never made public. I put up two shots of us and cropped them into close-ups rather than leave the wide shots that they originally were so there were shoulders showing. I had done it about half an hour before he was due home, to fill in the time waiting for him and some food.

I knew something was wrong as soon as he came upstairs as he had a routine of changing into casual clothes before eating. He dumped the food on the coffee table and went straight to the computer. 'Ah,' I thought, 'someone has already phoned him or said something to him, as he would have been travelling home when I put them up.' I heard his fist hit the office desk and he made a loud growling sound then he called me and asked, "What's this?"

I could not see what he was actually referring to or looking at until I walked in and sure enough he had the photos up that I just put there. He yelled, "I thought I told you and you agreed not to show these photos." I said, "I thought it was okay now as Mama is gone and they are such beautiful photos of us that I wanted to add them to my special memories album of us." I said, "Okay, I will take them off." So I immediately took them off and said, "It is okay, I have removed them, I am sorry for my mistake." Well it was on. He got up and came at me, belting my face from side to side yelling, "I am Muslim man. What you think people say?" I asked, "What is wrong with them? They are off Facebook now, you can check." They had only been there a half hour at most.

He continued to belt me, over and over again. I moved away but he came after me, no matter where I went, continually belting me. When I walked he tried to kick box me and trip me up. I was constantly moving around the room not knowing where I should go as we were upstairs. He was in a blind rage and the look on his face was death defying. I went back to the coffee table as it had been upended again and like the time before, I picked up the cups then thought that if I went downstairs away from him he might stop.

I was just saying, "I am sorry, I am sorry," but it made no difference. When I was on the landing at the top of the stairs he'd snatched the coffee cup out of my right hand so hard that it snapped the handle off and cut my finger open. He pushed me towards the stairs and I started falling down them. I was afraid of falling further and managed to grab the banister. My ankle twisted under me. For the first time in my life, my anger at this made me retaliate and I threw the glass in my other hand in his direction. Of course it missed him totally as he ducked. I then realised that my finger was bleeding quite badly and tried to get past him to go to the bathroom. He belted me again.

I stood at the sink, trying to stop the bleeding and he was still belting me. Suddenly, without me realising it, I had swung my right hand around and connected his cheek and yelled, "Stop hitting me!" I had knocked his glasses off which, damn it, fell to the floor and cracked. I thought, 'Shit! Now I will have to pay for them too and they were new as he was always breaking them.' With that, he said, "Right, now you are on your own, you can do what you want." I said, "I have been on my own all year, you have not cared about me at all." It was the wrong thing to say as he started belting me more. I went back into the main area and he followed, still belting and pushing me. The Achilles tendon in my ankle, which had already twisted on the stairs, went on me as he belted and shoved me again. I went down; the pain was insane and now I couldn't walk. He belted me some more then went down to the studio. I was in agony. My face was already turning black and purple and a black eye was forming. He was not satisfied until he drew blood when beating me.

I could not walk; the pain was horrendous as I tried to get to the bed. In the morning I awoke to see him standing in the office with tissue paper. He had his back to me and was carefully wrapping something up. I lay back down and soon afterwards he left and went out.

I got up and staggered on one foot to the walk-in wardrobe. I checked his pocket and the fancy watch was gone. The night before, the watch was still there as I checked each day since finding it. I knew where he

was going; she was obviously still in Bali. He came home later that day at sundown and didn't say a word. He could see my face and that I couldn't walk but just ignored me trying to get around. I was sure he would cancel my trip to this huge wedding by making up an excuse to the family but he didn't. We were leaving the next morning. I had taken photos of my face as a record because I now kept a daily diary on him and his movements and everything else in case I needed them at some stage. I had been advised to do this by the agent and later, her police chief business partner.

I'd packed the clothes I thought I would need but, like always, needed to check with him to make sure that not only were they suitable but at occasions like weddings and special events he would tell me what to wear. My choice between what I would like to wear or had chosen was never the preferred choice in his mind. He seemed to choose one particular ¾ length dress for everything. It was nice but now I had grown weary of it after having worn it to so many outings and occasions. I had all the Muslim clothes but he seldom liked to see me wearing them, even in front of his family. I asked him a few times why I had to take off what I was wearing but he'd just said, 'No, don't wear that.' The only time it seemed okay was when we went to his special Muslim organisation in the Renon named Asy-Syifa a very good organisation who help the poor and orphaned children, and teach the purity of the Holy Quran but then too, my dress was modified compared to all the women there, which used to make me feel out of place constantly and shamefully uncomfortable.

I had adapted the motto, 'Live by the tides for I am no longer the master of my own ship I tried not create stormy seas.' This is not my country, I must respect their culture and their ways and obey my husband; this is showing that I honour him, by being a good wife.

"A woman is like a tea bag – you never know how strong she is until she gets in hot water."

Eleanor Roosevelt

Morning came; I had to get on the motorbike with Hass, carrying our bag in this dreadful state. I had no idea how I was going to manage climbing the steps into the plane. It was so humiliating being exposed to the public in this condition. I had tried to cover my black and blue face with makeup but it was very difficult as both sides of my face were such a mass of injuries. My heart was crying. We moved up the queues in silence towards the boarding lounge. People were staring at me and I felt total embarrassment. I was hoping they were thinking I'd been in a motorbike accident or something similar.

It was a painful challenge just getting on the bus that took us out to the plane waiting on the tarmac. I looked up to the top of the steps that entered the plane thinking, brace yourself you are going to be very slow and hold everyone up who just wants to get on board. I tried to move as quickly as I could by hanging onto and using the railing to hoist myself up each step. I wondered, as I climbed, how crippled people manage on these aircrafts travelling between the islands of Indonesia; it must be terrible for them. Finally, seated in silence, my mind shot ahead to the arrival and what I was going to say when asked about my injuries as I knew my sister-in-law would want to know for sure. I had decided to avoid giving an answer as I was not one for lying to anyone.

We disembarked and waited for the luggage. Hass went and got a trolley, not that we needed it, he was strong and we only had a medium sized suitcase. "Here, sit," he said pointing to the trolley. I thought, 'I can't do

that,' but at his insistence I sat on the edge. He then said, "Sit there," as he started to wheel the trolley out. I tried to get up as this was not a good image for a western woman and I would never do this even for a joke. I felt like a complete fool and idiot sitting there like the beat up queen of nothing as I faced a sea of very respectable Muslim citizens. We had to wait for some time before being picked up by the family and the longer the wait, the more intimidated I became.

We dropped our luggage off at the family house where we were staying. They were all lovely and greeted me very warmly. I didn't know this part of the family. My sister-in-law was at the other venue preparing for the evening ahead of the first ceremony. A short time later we were escorted to there. It was a climb up more stairs to the area of the building that the event was being held in. I had no idea whatsoever what to expect. This was very different from Balinese ceremonies. I finally reached the top landing where many women were busy preparing for the event. There I met my sister-in-law who was a sweetie. She reached out and touched my face saying, "Why? What happened?" I flinched and pulled back with a little smile, not saying anything as my eyes scanned the faces staring at me. I dropped my eyes, trying to block out the questions on their faces. I tried desperately to find the wisdom within me, saying to myself, gather your strength, deep breath, courage and confidence,

"I will look fear in the face.
I lived through this horror
I can take the next thing that comes along
I must do the things I think I cannot do.
A wise passage of wisdom I had adapted
for myself from a great woman,"

Eleanor Roosevelt (1884-1962),
which stood firmly in my mind.

I was 'encouraged' to rest and have a sleep unlike the many times I had adapted to their way of life when I was a guest in their environment. I lay on the heavily carpeted area which had been prepared for the evening and slept solidly for an hour or so which gave me great relief and helped me to compose myself. I was woken up to eat some deliciously prepared food and sweets. We then returned to the house with the family. A group of women sat around with us to catch up on family in general but my face became the main topic before very long. Again my sister enquired, "What happened to your face?" I shrugged it off saying I would rather not talk about it, as this too is a condition of Islam; a wife should keep all private matters between her and her husband no matter whether good, bad or ugly. Well, that is what I read and that was, up until now, how I had always been with my relationships.

Smirking, Hass chipped in and said, "Go on, tell them." I said, "No." He told them and then said, "Go on, tell them." He had already done that saying he had 'slapped' me for doing it. They knew and could see this was no one-off slap as my face was the compelling evidence that they were viewing up close. Then she asked, "What happened to your foot?" Now it was very bruised and double its size, like someone with gout. I made the excuse that I fell over.

That evening I was in full view of hundreds of people. I had been left to sit by myself wherever I could squeeze in. Hass was nowhere to be seen so I went upstairs thinking that is where I should be, alongside him. Finally, when I found him sitting with the main party he indicated to me that there was no room for me to sit anywhere. I struggled back downstairs and thought, 'Please God, take me out of here, I can't take this.' I disappeared outside and went over the road to hide behind a car and have a much needed smoke. At this time it was my only salvation and comfort. Everyone was friendly to me but I could not converse with any of them as they spoke their own dialect. A few lovely ladies who were direct family came to my rescue at one point and hugged me, sat with me and took photos. I had piled on the makeup for the night; thank goodness for my experience in the film and TV industry and watching my makeup artist mates. They had taught me a few tricks

to hide bruising and marks. I called them into play which managed to make an improvement in hiding the worst. I just prayed the photos would not reveal my black eyes as I wore my contact lenses to try to look fresher.

I wondered what Hass would do come sleep time as we had been given a newly married daughter's bedroom to sleep in, which was very generous of them. It had a double bed and as he had not slept in our bed for many months but crashed on the lounge suite listening to his CB it was going to be interesting to see if he portrayed the married couple image for them all. When he took a shower I checked his phone, even though he had turned it off. He had spent a great deal of time distracted and walking off wherever we were to make or take a call. Sure enough, they had been full on with phone calls and text messages between them. That night, Hass actually slept in the bed which surprised me, although the following night he pretended he was hot and I found him sleeping on the garage floor. With night one down I thought I could handle the hundreds of people I had been told would be attending the ceremonies. However, the following night was to be at another venue with other guests participating in celebrating the wedding.

The day went casually by; he went out with family and I was left sitting in the house on my own for most of the day. I didn't appreciate this at all as people came and went from the house and I hadn't a clue who anyone was and could not converse with them. A few people could speak some English, the younger ones, but they were not there either. When Hass returned with the others he proceeded to massage my leg and foot in front of the family. I wondered if he had genuine remorse for what he had done to me, or if this was for show. He said, "I couldn't do this if I didn't feel something in my heart but I cannot massage under the foot." I never knew what that meant and I never said anything. My foot was huge with the bruising and swelling. I did not have any money or transport to go to a doctor to have it x-rayed the day before we left. There could have been a break but it would be too late by the time we got back to do much about it, even if I could find the money to do something.

Night came and I had to wear the same dress that I had worn the night before. I did my best to feel comfortable showing up in the same outfit while the family had changed several times into beautiful elaborate outfits as was their custom. On arrival at what looked like a ballroom because it was so large, I saw there were hundreds of parked cars. Hobbling along we walked towards the entrance. Everyone had to file in line down this very long carpeted foyer where many people stood waiting to enter the ballroom. It looked absolutely stunning with decorations and lots of colour. I walked alone; Hass was behind me until we got to the door, which gave me zero confidence. I had forced on a pair of heels which made my foot blow up like a balloon but I'd tried flat shoes and I could not walk in them at all.

We entered the room and I just wanted to shrivel up into nothingness as there sat hundreds of people. Oh dear God, just focus on the bride and groom ahead, was all I could think about. They were sweeties, so gentle and beautiful and that made my discomfort and pain a little easier to bear.

There was a group entertaining the crowd but after a while Hass was introduced and asked to play and sing a lot of great local songs for the mass of people attending the ceremony. He played a song I had learned to dance to, called Pocho Pocho; it has a real Portuguese flavour to it. I taught it to many tourists at resorts and restaurants while spending an evening amongst them. Hass indicated for me to get up and dance. I thought, 'Are you crazy or what? I can barely hobble, let alone dance. What is this, grand standing me for the world to see in this state?' Again I received a glare and head nod that said, 'Get up!' So I attempted to dance with my weight on the other foot as I moved. I sat down before the music had finished. Now, as if this wasn't enough, including all the photos and video shots with me in them, Hass began to play the opening bars of my song. I thought he was going to sing it but he repeated the intro and gave me a signal to get up and sing.

A million thoughts in a split second went racing through my mind. I looked at him reluctantly, but knew by his face that I had to do it, or else.

There I stood before the throng, microphone in hand, trying to codger not only courage but the emotion of my song, 'Mama's Heart.' It was received very well with a huge round of applause at the end but I was feeling nothing now, I was emotionally numb.

He sang the love song, Unchained Melody. Over the past year whenever he sung this, tears just fell down my cheeks and this evening was no different. The pain in my heart from what he was doing was tearing me apart and all my dreams were being shattered and cast to the wind. My brother-in-law had his video camera running at the time and he, being an intuitive man, had honed in on me during the song. I tried to control my emotions and pretend I didn't know the camera was on me. It's a hard thing to do when you understand filming so well and where the camera lens is pointed. I remember trying to look evasively at what was happening in the ballroom with people mingling with each other but I was glad when the night was over. The next day was nice with just his brother, wife and the two of us going to the town to have some traditional Makassar food. I really enjoyed the flavours and the tenderised beef.

It was not overly spiced, like so many places in Bali where I always had to be careful what I ate. A few years prior to this I had suddenly become so allergic to something that the doctors couldn't and still can't identify but it had caused me to go into anaphylactic shock three different times and nearly ended my life. Since then, I have had to carry an Epi-Pen injection with adrenalin, to be instantly administered, in my purse everywhere I go. This keeps me alive until, usually, an ambulance with life support arrives and takes me to hospital if I have an attack. If I have an attack it's a very scary thing for the people around me to witness. Mouth to mouth resuscitation does not work as my throat closes off completely. We set off back to Bali the following day. We arrived home in the evening and as we were hungry stopped in at one of the regular venues Hass sang at, for some food. His brother and wife gave us some money at the airport before leaving which was so very kind of them.

We finished eating but as normal Hass then got up and began playing the keyboard and singing while his male keyboard partner came and sat

down. He said hello to me and then he sat there, stunned, staring at my face but at the same time trying to pretend he was not shocked. While he was viewing my face he was trying to engage in polite conversation. I sat uneasily in my chair as I knew my makeup had rubbed off and my bruises were probably exposed. I excused myself and hobbled to the toilet. I tried to apply a bit of makeup but, feeling sick and exhausted, did not put much effort into it. I just wanted to go home but Hass continued to play, full of ego. Finally, we got home two hours after we had landed. A week later, my sister-in-law rang to say she and a group of ten women were landing in Bali to follow the bride and groom on their honeymoon and could all ten of them, including the bridal couple, stay with us? I said, "Well, we don't have ten beds but we could turn the studio into a sleeping area. The bridal couple can have the guest room but please realise that I have no food or money to buy any food."

It totally embarrassed me to have to say this to family but it wasn't a problem for them, so they came. During the day they were out and about and I did not go as my foot was still extremely bad. When Hass wasn't there they all asked me again what had happened so I told them, with the members who could speak English translating. I was reluctant at first but I could see by their eyes that they had a genuine concern for me. The women even said that I should have hit him back. I told them I did give him that one slap that was not deliberate but a reaction; they said, 'Good!' They asked if I still loved him and what I was going to do now. I had not told them about the women, only that I had not fallen and that he had pushed me down the stairs. They sat there aghast.

They moved to another house before their planned departure and I was sitting watching TV as Hass had gone to sing. A car tooted at the gate and, wondering who it was, I went out onto the verandah. I was surprised to see it was Hass's brother and sister in-law back with two other family members. My brother in-law was shocked to see my face and foot and on examining my foot asked if I had seen a doctor or had my foot x-rayed. I explained why not. He then asked for the story, which I told him, but I had made a slip-up saying there was another situation involving someone else but I would not say who or what gender. He

then made a slip-up talking about some other young woman with Hass. Jeez! Another one! I didn't know about her!

He then explained the reason they had come to Bali and said I was not to tell. He said they had been with my sister in-law's husband (the second eldest brother) who could not join them in Bali because of work back in Sulawesi, where we had just been. He had rung her that day and told her to bring me money. She held out her hand and tried to put it in mine saying, "This is for you and you must not give 1 rupiah to him." The other brother sitting there said the same thing. Then they left as they wanted to go before Hass was due home. I was overcome with gratitude at their kindness. I tried to refuse it but they would not have a bar of this. I cried, they cried. They apologised for what Hass had done to me.

Everything returned to how it had been before going away and I went to his gigs in Kuta again. Meanwhile, I rang a person I got to know when he had bought something from me. He happened to be an ex Australian CIB detective and was now living in Bali. I thought he may be able to help me find a buyer in Bali for the villa. I told him my circumstances and he gave me two names of people who could possibly help me get it sold. They were in real estate in Bali. I rang the woman first and spoke with her. Though Indonesian, she spoke some English.

She and her partner came to the villa to have a look and give me their conditions of sale. I read through it and told Hass I had, with his knowledge, arranged to meet them at the venue where he was singing as I had to take them all the documents required for selling. I was still black and blue and could not walk properly even though two weeks had passed. Hass did not like these people and thought they were there just to trick us and steal the property from me. Little did he know that they already knew my circumstances and only I knew that her business partner was also high up in the police force. When they saw the state of me, and after Hass had started singing, they offered me a 'safe house' they could take me to. I said no, because I knew that if I left the property and him I would lose the lot!!! I was going nowhere until the property

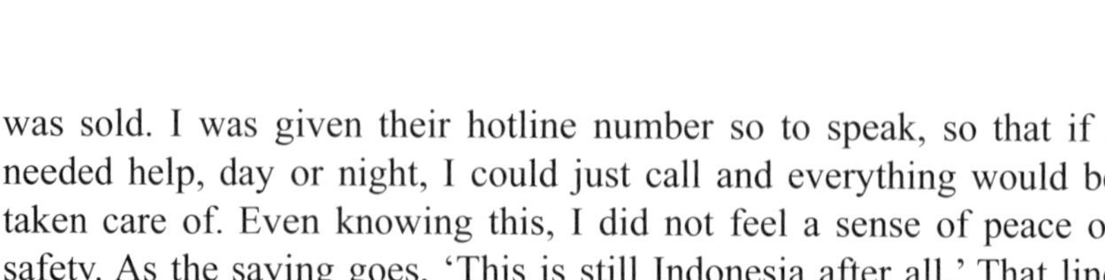

was sold. I was given their hotline number so to speak, so that if I needed help, day or night, I could just call and everything would be taken care of. Even knowing this, I did not feel a sense of peace or safety. As the saying goes, 'This is still Indonesia after all.' That line would play in my head many times but I very much appreciated their kind help.

I had managed to painfully struggle up my little stony road to the small local shop at the corner to buy a packet of cigarettes. The woman who had been my neighbour from 2005 to October 2010 and who I had only waved to but never had a conversation with, was coming down our road. She stopped when she saw my condition and offered me a lift for the 1,000 yards or so to my gate. She saw my state and my face and said that if I ever needed to chat or anything to come down to her place. A short time after that, I paid her a visit when Hass went to sing.

She asked me to join her for some food. I accepted gratefully as I had had very little food to eat. From that evening on, we became good friends. I finally had a friend and neighbour. I had never been one to get involved with neighbours, except to say hello or help if they needed it. She ended up, over the next two years, being my saving grace in more ways than one. Thank you, God.

My two daughters were also my saving grace as they knew everything that was going on because we kept in touch via email and phone calls and they had seen the photos of the abuse I was suffering. Words don't describe the anger they felt towards Hass as they were now giving me what support they could. They would send a parcel of food and necessaries to me at different times and put a little money in my bank account when they could as they guessed I wasn't eating and had no money. I only had what I managed to get from selling my belongings when I could. There was one other person in Bali who I shall keep anonymous and just call that person brave heart. That person knows who they are, should they read this book.

I had heard madam and Hass, (which is short for his full name; he had another abbreviation of his name for singing, and an alias on the CB radio) at different times from each other, discussing marriage on the network with their buddies. I had recorded them both and had it all translated to confirm what they were saying. Now I was really panicking. How could they do this? When? He said he planned on having two wives and laughed. He was asked if he was afraid of what could happen and he'd said yes. When my friend who was translating told me this I said, "He may think he is going to have two wives but not while he is married to me." If a man has more than one wife the first wife must give permission in writing and he can only do this by the law of Islam if he can support both wives equally in 'every' respect. He was not supporting me, so how was he going to manage two wives? It was not going to happen!! Maybe in another lifetime but not while I was around. Christmas came and went with me tending my gardens. I could no longer even do any painting as there were no canvases or paints left. That was disheartening, as I loved to paint and see what emerged at the end of a piece. You see, I cannot draw, due to dyslexia. I see the vision in my head and know what I want to do but my brain and hand have a disconnection on drawing lines and shapes and copying things. Most of my artwork is abstract in one form or another, or it just reveals itself when I am finished the piece in my own special style.

Mystic Shadows 3D

Tree Whispers, Stop Poverty

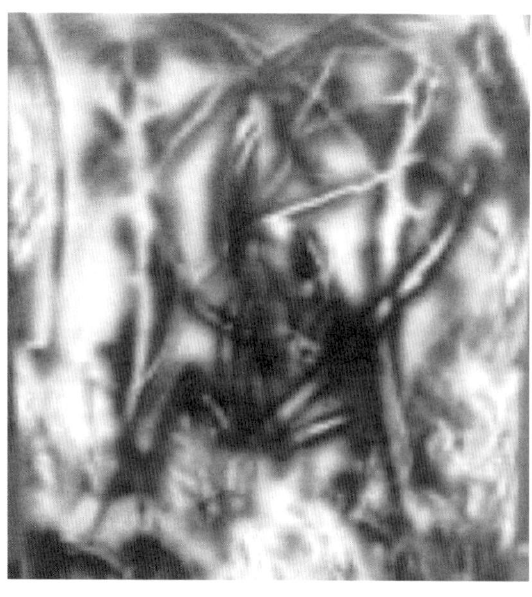

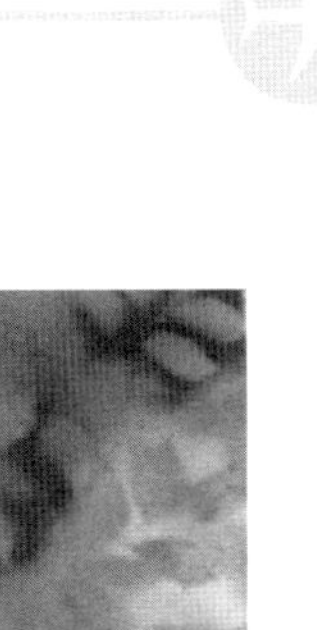

Direct Line To The Sky.

The interesting thing however, is that with some of my art I use my own secret technique to discover images within my work. Once I see what has evolved I am able to develop it from there. These images are not by my hand and brush stroke, they just come through.

This fascinates me and those who see them; my poorer work is when I try to paint the 'correct way.' I have disappointment and frustration in comparison. I only started trying to paint after arriving in Bali. Before that, I had been doing and loving different types of craft work, e.g. making bush walking sticks and bark paintings. I always liked to try new skills and push my own boundaries to see who I was.

My dear colleague and mate said to me, "It is as though you have a connection with the sky. I have only met two people in my life with this special gift." Such a generous thought coming from him.

"I've come to believe that each of us has a personal calling that's as unique as a fingerprint – and that the best way to succeed is to discover what you love and then find a way to offer it to others in the form of service, working hard and also allowing the energy of the universe to lead you."

Oprah Winfrey

Chapter Eight

My Battle for Survival

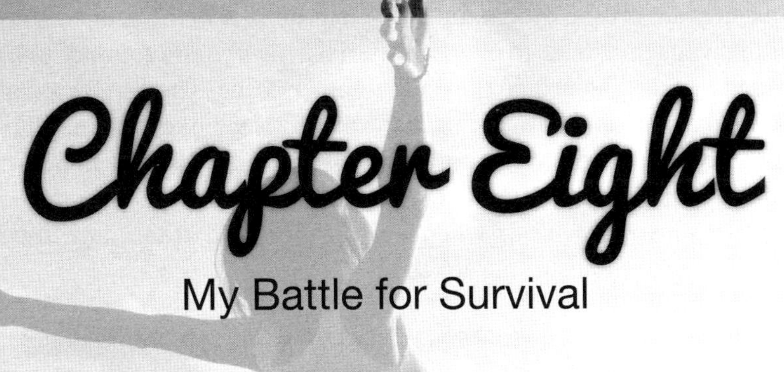

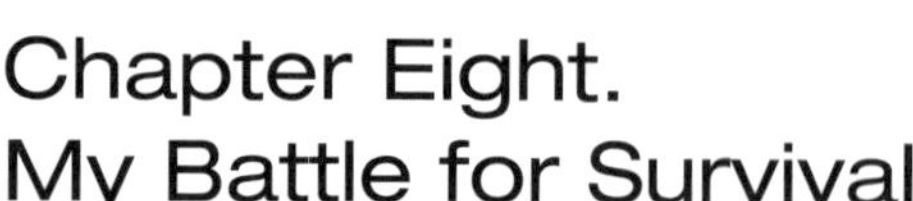

Chapter Eight. My Battle for Survival

I constantly advertised things for sale. I had to. It is in the grimmest of times that you learn to let go of your material treasures and commodities, they are not fulfilling nor do they add to inner peace. They are external comforts that we gather around us in the comforts we like to have. They do not teach us boundaries, humility, or wisdom; those are the things in life that are irreplaceable and that sustain our very existence. It is those things that move on with us when we pass over and at the same time remain within the souls of our loved ones.

To me, life is about love, honesty, respect, honour, trust, thankfulness, compassion, giving, sharing, honouring nature and acknowledging our blessings and gifts from above.

It was the 31st of December and we were entering into 2011. We left home in the morning to travel to the other rural area of Bali, away from where we lived. We were to meet up with the rest of the band not far from home and travel together. On arriving early and waiting in the humid heat and blistering sun for a while, Hass decided we would go ahead on our own. We had his entertainment clothes with us and my outfit. I always dressed up for this occasion in a long evening gown but this night I chose to wear a knee length dress for a change. Other years I had sat in corridors at resorts or far away and off to the side, in an evening gown, not being able to enter the area where everyone celebrated until the end. I wondered where I would have to be on this occasion. It didn't matter, at least I was not sitting alone at home and I could hear the music.

We arrived at the venue first and the sound and stage was still being set up and tested. Hass said he wanted to go and do sholat as it was Friday. He always went to male communal prayers on a Friday. This usually only took fifteen minutes and it was approximately 1pm. He said there was a Mosque close by, and left. He was gone for about two and a

half hours. Meanwhile, the band had arrived and asked where he was. I figured he was either meeting up with or seeing some old friends as he had lived in this area years ago. I tried ringing but his phone was off so I sent a text message. Eventually he turned up and we went to a room that the resort had allocated for the band. For the first time since I had managed 'our band' a proper suite had been given to the band for them to relax and shower in. I was impressed.

It was a very pleasant surprise as the band which had two ladies singing, one of whom I had not met before, also welcomed me, including the guys, and they invited me to be part of the group while waiting to perform that night. I was invited to join them for a meal and share soft drinks and coffee. Everyone chilled out and told stories; it was nice.

It was time for everyone to be on stage; the evening had begun. It was 6:30pm. I went upstairs with them and quietly sat in a lounge area where you could only hear the band. It was the band, during the first break, that said, 'Come upstairs with us. When we go back on there are chairs and a table you can sit at.' I thanked them very much. It was great, I could see the band performing, watch the guests enjoying the night and lo and behold the staff came over and asked if I would like champagne. I felt quite blessed. My glass was also topped up during the evening. Guests came over and chatted with me and later in the night some guests even got me up to dance with them. Yeah.

The New Year was seen in by all in the jolliest of ways. People from countries in Europe, Australia and Asia were in Bali each year. One lovely lady came over to chat with me. She was middle aged and she said she was sad as she had recently lost her husband of forty years and the family had asked her to come away with them. She had tears in her eyes and I gave her a big hug. She said to me you look very sad yourself and asked why I was on my own and not sitting with the other guests. I explained that my husband was the singer. He had just finished singing Unchained Melody and I had just wiped my own tears away when she came over. She gave me a hug. We had a dance together and then she left.

The band was great. Hass was as wonderful as ever. I still remained his faithful #1 groupie!! Guests just wanted them to keep on playing past the elected time for them to stop. This would normally be around 1 or 2 am depending on the venue. Hass came off stage and towards me and gave me a really nice kiss, the way it used to be, and he said Happy New Year. We looked at each other then kissed twice more; This was the old days revisited; of the romantic lingering kisses. He stood there looking straight into my eyes without saying anything further. I didn't know what that meant and I just smiled at him.

We gathered our belongings along with the rest of the band and headed for home. The main streets were quiet by this stage but there would have been raging parties going on in the Kuta streets for sure. We had been at Nusa Dua. We were starving but the only place open was a local café that we used to go to when we lived in the Renon area. After having some food we headed for home. The next day was quiet with nothing special happening.

I was hoping that in the New Year things might go back to happier times. We had a time of intimacy after I left a note for him saying, 'Let us put the past behind us and make love.' It was sexual, as I will put it, but different insofar as I found him to be unusually dominant, which he was not as a rule. My hopes of a new beginning fell by the wayside within days. He returned to his usual non communicative self except if he wanted something. He had not yet received the full payment for New Years Eve and said it would be another couple of weeks.

I was waiting for the money to pay the electricity bill and buy some food. When he finally got the money he said he wanted to take half of it to buy this CB system as his friends on the radio could not hear him properly. I said, "But there are bills to pay." He was paid and he took half the money. I asked him where this new system was that he had just paid for and he said he still had more to pay. I was pissed off. He did give me what was left but it was now nowhere near enough to pay the electricity bill. I asked him to ask the woman I loaned the one million rupiah to, if she could please pay it back as we needed it. (Inwardly I knew what the answer would be, as I had still not been paid or heard a word from her.)

I had to try and sell something immediately, no matter how much I had to drop the price. I managed to sell one of my amazing antique lounge suites that I had bought when I won a bit of money on gold lotto in Australia. It was worth many thousands of dollars. My French neighbour had wanted to buy it before so I approached him to see if he still wanted it. He did, but as he was short of money too I accepted his offer, which was very little in comparison to its real value. I took it. I had enough to pay the electricity for the next couple of months and the rest went to pay the woman who had given me the loan plus an installment on my Australian credit cards. My coffers were empty again.

In February, Hass was due to get his January payment for singing with his usual band. He said he wanted half of that to pay the balance owing on this confounded CB system. My dismay was shrugged off and now, being afraid of him, I tried not to antagonise him in any situation, small or great, even though I knew and felt this was unjust. I saw very little of his earnings. He had just earned an amount that would have given us food and paid bills but it was all gone. It was all I could do to try and make a pathetic meal out of nothing or wait endless hours for him to come home with a token of food. I kept vigilance on his pockets.

Meanwhile, my darling daughter had sent me a message to say she had deposited something in my bank account so I could buy some food and things for myself. I was ever so grateful. It took a couple of days to come through. I found Hass had 500,000 rupiah stashed in his pocket and wondered where it had come from. Suddenly I could feel the rage welling up inside me at the thought of my daughter, who was working so hard, sending money for me to buy food while this shit had money and was hiding it from me. I had spent my entire capital on trying to provide and support a good life for us and many others and it had come down to this. I debated with myself about tackling him on it but thought wiser of it and figured that if I exposed my findings he would go underground and I wouldn't be able to keep track of anything going on; it was for my own protection. I shut my mouth.

Instead, I told him my daughter had sent some money to buy food thinking it would give him an opportunity to say he had some but he

was not forthcoming at all. I asked him to take me to the supermarket. I withdrew some of the money that she had given me and thought I had better leave some there. He had added stuff to the cart but I tried to focus on what was needed. The checkout operator was putting the goods through and I watched it add up. I realised I had not withdrawn enough money and said to Hass that I would have to go and get more money from the ATM. He just stood there in silence. Back I came and again I saw that I still needed some more and went back. Inside, I was furious; knowing there was this money tucked away in his pocket just made me sick.

I wanted to scream at him. When the final tally came through I had taken all the money from my account and I looked at him because I was still 5,000 rupiah (about $1) short. I said, "You have 5,000 in your wallet." He glared at me and gave up the 5,000 rupiah. Anger and rage does not describe what I was feeling let alone the feeling of humiliation again in front of many western tourists in the queue. .

I tried to remember where he said he had been in the last day or so, as I now kept a day to day diary about him. I remembered he said he was going to his brother's house the day before. I thought, 'Bugger it, I will text him and ask him if he gave Hass any money.'

" Always go with the choice that scares you the most, because that's the one that is going to require the most from you."

Caroline Myss

Thank God his brother was honest with me. He replied that he had given him 500,000 rupiah. I asked what it was for and his reply was, "I don't know, for love!!!!" He included the information that Hass had also gone to his other brother and asked for 300,000 rupiah. I thanked him. I could not figure out what the hell was going on or why he would ask them for money as he told me he had never asked anyone for money, ever, way back when I first got to know him.

The 500,000 rupiah was gone and then suddenly the 300,000 rupiah appeared and then disappeared within days of each other. There was no sign of the CB radio system or anything else. I had found, stashed in a cupboard in the garage, a brand new Muslim style shirt which was expensive as it still had the price tag on it as well as a pair of women's sandals. I took the shirt and sandals inside and waited for him to come home. I said, "I happened to look in the cupboard and found these." "Oh," he said, "the sister in-law had bought it for him when he took them shopping in a hired car." I put the sandals on my feet and he said, "They are not for you, why would you wear them?" Then he said they belonged to her, she also bought them and forgot them. Mmm. Later in the week I asked where the sandals were and he said he already sent them to her. I always forgot to ask her if she got them. I heard on the CB that something was coming up, some kind of party or event but a lot of talk was coded.

I learned that 'they' were out shopping together. The location of the event was in the Sanur/Renon area but again they coded its exact location. I thought something was fishy. I watched him come and go as he was hardly home.

Our wedding anniversary was coming up at this time and as usual I posted it on Facebook with a little comment. It passed without a word from him when I said, "It's our anniversary today (the 12th February 2012,). I think I muttered a sarcastic, "Well happy anniversary to me," when he had done his usual walk away in silence. A couple of weeks later I learned from sources that they had secretly got married! the day after our wedding anniversary on the 13th February 2011 'his mistress'

or should I say his wife! had actually changed her status and posted on fb that she had re-'married' 13th February 2011. . This news totally blew me away. How could I find out for sure? He had started calling her Ma in his text messages and she constantly, not only on CB radio but also in text messages, called him Papa. She was asking his permission to go places in the text messages which is done if you're married. Here He was still living at home with me beating and starving me for the past year, while in adulteress illegal marriage to her. I figured they were both very demented people as it was a huge joke amongst them and their seedy friends. Although he was in the house some of the day or night he spent most of his time either sleeping or on the CB radio in the studio. It was ghastly.

The next thing I noticed, one day when I went into the large bathroom, was that he was sitting in the twin bath shower literally scrubbing his underwear with a brush. I said, "I'll do that," (as I always did the washing) "why are you washing your underwear?" I must add that up until now he was impeccably clean in this department. He said sharply, "Can't I wash my own clothes?" "Well, of course you can," I replied and went out. I thought maybe he had had an accident or something and didn't want me to have to fix it. But no, that was not the case because from then on I would find, the majority of the time, either he had been scrubbing them clean or they would be hidden in pockets in the wardrobe.

It was fairly obvious from this point on. Even after his 'scrubbing,' this weird glue-like mark would remain. One time when I found his underwear deep in the wash basket I tried to wash them clean but whatever this stuff was just would not come off. This was beyond me, I could not imagine what was going on and I wasn't up to speed on all this stuff.

I realise it is very tacky for me to even mention this but it was part of the drastic change that had occurred in all his characteristics since being involved with this woman. I could not believe how someone, in a very short space of time, had done a complete 360 degree turn from

the person I knew or thought I knew. I only went to hear him singing a few more times but after being ready to go and yet again to be told to stay home, I figured it was the last time I would attempt it. I was like a prisoner in my own home now. I had no transport, day or evening. No money, although I continued to sell stuff, and no food most of the time. Whatever I got went to the woman who had loaned me the money for the villa.

I had gone to Bali and although I grieved as a person my body had recovered somewhat and outwardly I looked in pretty good shape. I had always kept a good physical appearance due to years of gymnastics, athletics, playing squash, teaching aerobics and working on the property.

But now my body had succumbed to dropping a full stone in weight from the lack of food and stress. My face was drawn and thin. People did not recognise me any more and it used to make me cry. I would say hi to people on Facebook and I would get the reply, 'Who are you?" That was hard to take.

My daughters were both so worried about me that one was coming back to visit me. She had been there three times before and we had a great time, the three of us. My other daughter had never been but was coming the following month. I had said to them, "Please, if you come, you are not to let on what you know as it will put me at risk." A tall request to ask of your daughters when they are so worried. I said, "If you can't do this it is better if you don't come."

The day my daughter was arriving I asked Hass to drop me off at the airport to meet her as he already had some plans. She had arranged to take a rental car from the airport. We jumped in that and decided to go for lunch in Sanur. Hass joined us. We had a nice meal which she paid for, bless her. We picked up a few groceries and headed for home. I was really concerned about how this was all going to go and I tried to act like normal. She was different in her approach to Hass and he noticed it straight away although it wasn't much. He asked me if she was angry with him. I had to lie and say, "No, she is just tired."

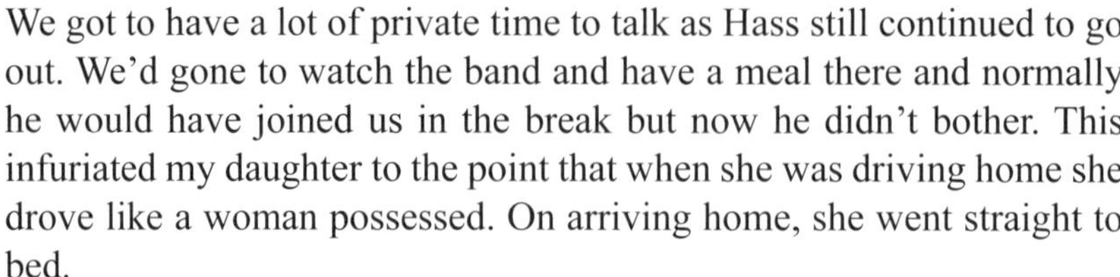

We got to have a lot of private time to talk as Hass still continued to go out. We'd gone to watch the band and have a meal there and normally he would have joined us in the break but now he didn't bother. This infuriated my daughter to the point that when she was driving home she drove like a woman possessed. On arriving home, she went straight to bed.

A couple of days later he said he was going to the transmitter station on top of the mountain with his mates. We went and spent girly time together and watched movies that evening as he had still not returned. I tried to contact him but his phone was switched off or not available. I waited until the early hours of the morning but he had still not shown up and I had heard nothing. By 5am I was worried that he may have had an accident as the road was dangerous and you can die on the roads of Bali in a split second, especially on a motorbike.

I woke my daughter and said, "He isn't home, I hope he hasn't had an accident." She was not happy with me because I had woken her. I went back upstairs and sent yet another message to Hass saying I was about to go to the hospitals to see if he had been admitted to any of them.

Suddenly I got a message saying, 'Sorry I go to the other side of Bali with friend and coming home now.' My concern turned into anger, how dare he do this to me while my daughter was here, giving us food and worrying about me.

When Hass arrived home at 7.30am I told him I was not happy and asked why he went to the other side of Bali without at least contacting me. I got the stories, including one that his mate was drunk and couldn't drive back. I thought, 'Since when weren't you capable of driving?' He became very aggressive to the point where he could have smacked me one. He would not dare while my daughter was there and if he did I had great fear for her as she would never again stand by and watch another man hit me. My daughter appeared upstairs as she would undoubtedly have heard our raised voices. She sat down and immediately said to him, "Do we have a problem?" He said, "No, your mother is not happy

with what I did." She said, "Well, it does not make me happy when my mother wakes me at the crack of dawn to say you are not home."

He then went into one of his famous speeches of how he would never cross the line or have any other woman, that I was the only woman he would have and so on. I sat there listening to this shit running off his tongue. Thank God she never said anything. She went back downstairs and by now it was about 11am. He had gone to have a shower and his phone rang. I went to look at it but accidently pressed the end call button. Oh hell. The next thing she sent him a message saying she was meeting her uncle for lunch and asked what he was doing and did he want to join them? If he did not answer with his permission she would go on her own. I wanted to answer the bitch E.C.H. and say, "How dare you! Leave my husband alone." I despised this woman with no morals. She would have known my daughter was there; in fact he probably hadn't gone with this phantom mate but been shacking up with her. Going by what I learned about their secret marriage, my scum-bag husband had married her three days before my daughter arrived.

He had her listed in his phone several times with all these alias names and numbers. ECH was one of them which turned out to be the initials of her name. He listed her under male friends but all had the same number and she had other numbers as well.

My daughter left and a month later my other daughter arrived. Hass was supposed to take me to the airport at a certain time to meet them. He had arranged to go to some grand opening of one of his female friends. I was not invited but I knew he had taken 'someone' with him on his motorbike when he returned home to finally pick me up. He was late and we were just leaving home as her plane was supposed to land. I was furious as I had been messaging him to get home. Hass greeted them with me. I had not seen my daughter for six years so it was a teary greeting. She was shocked to see my condition.

She too, hired a car but I drove it as she would never have handled Bali traffic. She freaked out just being a passenger. We had arranged to meet

Hass at the same place we'd had a meal with my other daughter. After the meal we went to the supermarket and the girls bought some supplies for the house, as in food.

We settled in at home and sat by the pool for our first catch up. Hass went into the studio and actually played some music. The first day was reasonably pleasant. In the morning they wanted to go and look around Ubud, an area I really liked. We strolled around, the girls buying a few items here and there and then we went for lunch. Again my daughter paid for us. Hass was singing that night so we were able to catch up and talk. I begged her to stay calm in his presence as it would make it very difficult for me if she didn't. She understandably found this difficult after having seen the photos of the beatings. I had hidden this completely from everyone for so long but I could not deceive them any longer and pretend that things were great on the island of the Gods; paradise. I had the worst nightmare ever, someone was trying to kill me they couldn't strangle me in the bed so they had forced my head through the door and my neck was being wrung like a piece of wet washing as it stretched like blue tack. It was so real I had let out this gut wrenching groaning sound that not only woke the girls but the neighbours heard me. I knew I had to get out of Bali and as soon as possible. I still recall it so vividly even now.

For some this is what it was and is, paradise, as they have a network of western social friends. But I spoke to some business people while trying to sell the property and who had shown interest and they said that even after thirteen years of struggling with business, it was far from paradise and every day was a roller coaster ride of negotiations, pay outs and working with the local people. Even when you can speak the language it is still a constant battle of miscommunication. You can show, describe, explain and check if they understand and they will say yes, yes and still go off and do it their way. I had been told this by many people.

It costs a fortune to set up a business or company there and can take years before all the legal documents are finalised, meanwhile your bank account is left with a gaping hole in it. Taxes are huge and you are never

seen as the owner of your own business. Like trying to acquire land, there has to be a local heading the company or at least be a director of it.

As time went on with my daughter and her friends staying it became more difficult for her to contain her anger and emotions but overall she was handling it well. We went to the venue where Hass was singing and they got to watch him perform. Like me and anyone who heard him sing, they loved his voice. I got up and sang the song I had written for my children and she was blown away. Firstly, she had never really heard me 'sing' before, not like that. She cried when hearing the lyrics and when I sat down she said, "Mum, that was amazing!" The song is called Mama's Heart.

One time when Hass and I were out just seeing his muso friends at resorts, he got me to sing it. On this particular night there were a couple of Aussie guys (who looked like businessmen) heading back towards their room but instead, they came into the bar to listen to me sing. When I finished I quietly went and sat down and they came over and said, "That was fantastic! Are you the resident singer?" I said, "Hell no, I am not a singer, my husband is the singer." They said, "Well, we stopped in to listen to you as we thought you were so don't underestimate yourself or sell yourself short, you are a great singer." I was shocked but felt good at the same time as this was a huge compliment and confidence booster for me.

We took the girls on a bit of a tour around for another couple of days and then it was time for them to go. It had been great to have both my daughters come and visit, one after the other as it gave me hope and lifted my spirits. I was sad to see them go and had no idea when I would be with them again. All I could do was focus on selling the property and hope this would change the course of my life, one way or the other. I was in God's hands.

It was so hard to sit there at night when Hass came home from singing and watch him playing on the CB radio while texting her. He would play love songs like, 'Hello,' 'Unchained Melody,' etc. He would have the CB jammed so nobody could interrupt. I would ask him what he was doing and he would just say in an unfriendly tone, nobody's on air and continue, followed by him texting her again at the end of the songs. He sure knew how to drive home pain and cut your heart with a knife.

I was pretty sure at one stage that she was impersonating me somehow and using my name as it became a joke on the airway. This woman was using my name with a certain guy she was speaking to but he fouled up during the conversation and called her by her real name, which she instantly replied to. They both laughed, then after someone else gave the coded interruption he quickly reverted back to the other name, which again was the same as mine. I asked my husband who this other Sandy in the network was and he switched off the CB with a typical excuse, but there was someone with my name. If they are Indonesian it is pronounced Sendy. I wondered if she was using my name to pass herself off as his wife with some legal documents or doing something to cover their illegal marriage. This is what my intuition was telling me at least. Thank God I have never been into mind games and childish antagonism. I tried to keep encouraging myself to focus on survival and my own personal responsibility.

"You may encounter many defeats, but you must not be defeated. In fact, it may be necessary to encounter the defeats so that you can know who you are, what you can rise from and how you can still come out of it."

Maya Angelou (Famous African Singer)

I was feeling extremely weak, both mentally and emotionally, but I had decided to try and keep my head high and retain my honour and belief in myself and what I stood for; truth, honour and humility. I tried very hard not to become paranoid by events and what was going on, as I know it is very easy to slip into this without realising it. You fight to survive, but I could not just turn a blind eye as I relied solely on myself for protection. I never want any other woman to go through what I have been subjected to and others who have met similar situations as myself living there.

Chapter Nine

Surviving on Instinct and Intuition

Chapter Nine.
Surviving on Instinct and Intuition

I was now often finding money hidden and could not work out where this extra cash was coming from as Hass was not doing any extra singing and I knew how much he earned at each place. Although there was no food of any substance in the house he never came forth about the money and it would be gone within a few days of it being there.

I kept on selling stuff even if it meant getting 200,000 rpt which is about $20. Even though he had this hidden stash he would come and get money from me for phone cards, petrol and whatever else. He was constantly out and generally came home in the early hours of the morning after singing. I would wait for him to bring food home with him and this would be the only food I would have in a 24 hour period.

I was blessed to have two neighbours who kept a close eye on me and where I could find shelter at any time if necessary. I will never forget them.

Hass had received a booking from someone and it meant going to his childhood island to sing at some wedding. There would be artists from Jakarta there as well. His airline ticket and hotel or motel room was being paid for. He could not tell me how much he would get paid for the event and gave a guesstimated figure to me. This meant he would have to cancel his regular work in Bali for at least three days.

Normally, if you were a guest performer at a wedding you got paid well, it was similar to or more than the pay for New Years Eve, depending on negotiations in many cases. The day came when Hass was supposed to leave. He came home to pack as the flight was just a few hours away. He had played with his wedding ring for the past year. Sometimes he would wear it, other times not, sometimes he would wear it on the other finger, or swap and change it within the day. This day was one of the times he'd gone out without it. It lay on the bathroom vanity. This used

to really bug me for reasons I am sure you will understand, given his daily extramarital life.

I took the ring in a moment of frustration and when he came home to pack he asked me, while sitting on the floor packing his suitcase, "My ring, where did I put it? I was wearing it this morning." I had been told so many lies on a daily basis that I thought, 'don't suck it up any more,' so I just casually said, "Bullshit, you weren't wearing it, you left it in the bathroom when you got dressed to go out." I held out his ring to him. Well in the flick of an eyelid he was on his feet.

Aggressively he faced me, "What you say?" "I said bullshit …" but got nothing else out as the whack went across my face. He snatched the ring from me and threw it hurtling across the floor. He was yelling at me and I thought, 'quick, get away from him or you are in for another dose like before.'

He went back to packing and monitoring his phone which he had put in the wardrobe with him. I sat in the lounge and he came across to give me a bit more of a beating when suddenly his phone rang. He ran into the walk-in cupboard and answered in a hushed voice then was talking. I thought it was strange, so snuck up to hear him saying, "Just wear your chocolate top," but of course in Indonesian. Of course, I instantly thought she was going with him or meeting him there from her island; at that point I was not sure if she was in Bali or back in Lombok.

I had 200,000 rupiah which I gave him as we had nothing else, or so I thought, but he'd had money in the hidden pocket.

I checked when he left and he had taken it with him. I had no money. I had no food and no transport as usual. He had said he'd be gone for three days but did not have a return ticket. He said the organiser would give it to him in Kupang. He had taken his bike (not that I could ride one) and was parking it at a friend's place, close to the airport. When I opened the gate for him to go he actually gave me a pleasant kiss, which threw me as he had not come near me affectionately since our intimate

time just after New Year's Day. He was gone. My lip and above my lip was already turning black and blue.

By the third day I had run out of drinking water and could not even find enough coins to go up the road to buy a small bottle. I had never drunk our deep well water as my stomach was very sensitive and I got stomach problems very easy. I had to boil this and felt it should be safe as this was what I had learned years ago while working and living in the bush and teaching survival skills to school children, adults and homeless youth back home. I had a few slices of bread and a small amount of jam left in a bottle so I had been eating a slice a day. That was my food.

While Hass was away he actually rang and sent me text messages, which had become extremely unusual for him. He still didn't know when he was coming back or if he did he was not saying. He finally returned five days after performing for the one evening. I figured he would catch up with family and old friends but strangely, he told me he didn't go visiting and just stayed at the motel. I found this hard to believe as he loved to spend time with everyone.

He rang from the airport and asked if I had eaten. I said, "You know I haven't eaten for five days so yes, please bring some food home." He seemed okay when he got home and when he got off his motorbike and said, 'Hello.' Then he looked at my face and asked, "What happened?" He had obviously forgotten that he had belted me before he left. I just looked at him and he quickly dismissed the conversation.

He gave me 1 million rpt and said he got just more than that but would have to keep it to give to the friend he had borrowed money from before going to the airport. He was crying poor while he was away, saying that he had nothing but I thought, 'Where did the money go that I gave you?' and I knew he'd taken his hidden stash, so in actual fact, if he was just buying snacks for lunch at local cafes he should have had plenty. There were no photos of this event like was normal and while he did enjoy mixing with the artist from Jakarta he had very little to say about

his trip which again, in the past he would have elaborated on and talked about for hours.

He had been given some special smoked meat which was delicious and a few special bottles of chilli which we loved. Family would sometimes bring some back for us because you couldn't get it in Bali. I proceeded to put it in the fridge thinking, 'Great, we have some meat.' He stopped me and said, "This is for us and this I give to my friend who loaned me the money." I thought that was cool and understood. He divided it in half. The next day he supposedly took the meat to his friend in Kuta.

When he returned home that evening I checked the areas where he stashed things away and I found this receipt. He had been careless and left it on the shelf just under some underwear. It was a receipt for having sent, by express to madam, the meat and chilli. He had not gone to his friend in Kuta at all, he had sent it to her in Lombok. Here I had starved for the past five days, had a fat lip and she was receiving the food from my mouth. I was silently enraged. I photographed the receipt and put it back.

His continual lies were getting to me; he had become a compulsive liar in the extreme and even though he knew I had studied body language and the combinations, he did not even consider this at any point and thought that I would just believe what he said. I had basically never questioned anything he had told me since I had known him but in those days I did not have to watch everything, or so I thought. Now I was beginning to realise that maybe I had been coerced and manipulated right from the start. That was a thought which led me to wonder if I really could have been that vulnerable and susceptible to allow this to happen to me.

I had tuned into the CB radio while Hass was out and I was more infuriated to hear 'their' buddies gossiping and laughing because he had sent her sapi (meat) as a present. Even though he was a bastard to me now, I still loved him and anyone laughing at him really upset me. I thought, 'That bitch is making a laughing stock of him and little

does he know that she is sharing everything with the world about them. Ungrateful cow!' If he knew she was doing this and that she was making a fool of him, it would have hurt him greatly. Whenever he had brought something home for me, no matter how small, I appreciated the thought and his efforts. I so wanted to ring this woman and let loose on her but I knew it would only be of further detriment to me and I would pay a heavy price. I found other receipts over the next couple of months for clothing and gifts Hass had sent her. I just kept recordings and photo records should I ever need them.

Somehow I had lost my key to the padlock on the gate. I never went anywhere so I don't know how I could have done that. I could no longer get out by going to visit my neighbour or walk to the beach. I'd told Hass it was lost and he needed to get another key cut for me. This never happened. I was locked in whenever he was out now. After a month, one evening when my friend invited me to come and eat something, I climbed the gate which was six foot high but it was a 3 metre wall in total and I'm only 162cm tall. It was not so bad getting over it to go out as I would first climb up the water fountain then jump down the other side onto the roadway. Getting back was a challenge. I did this for about another month. Hass had a key to the padlock but always took it with him and when he came home I would open the little hand door to get the key from him to unlock it.

I was doing some tidying up in the office one day and, like before, I had tried all the keys that looked as if they might fit the padlock, on the off chance one of them would work. I found some old keys in a container and thought one looked like the padlock key or much like the one I'd had, so I went down to the gate. Hey presto! It opened the padlock. Yeah freedom! I quickly and excitedly went down to my neighbour. I said nothing to Hass. After a couple of weeks I thought, 'Sod it, let him wonder how I managed to get a key,' as I had been nowhere. So, I opened the gate for him but he never said a word. A few people had come to look at the property and I would get my hopes up and then they would be dashed as nothing was serious.

Hass was now disappearing overnight and it got to the point where he was not turning up to sing for some of his bookings. He would not contact me to say where he was or when he would be home. I would get a call from the band leader asking where he was and that was how I learned he had not shown up. He was now becoming unprofessional for a person so experienced and who used to call others out to me for being this way.

He was now involved in organising a reunion for his university. I had long since worked out that life to him was just a game. Several times he had told me he didn't like problems. None of us do but that is what you get in life, the highs and the lows and you work through them.

Not him, his motto was, 'Don't put any problem or allow any problem to get inside your head to disturb you,' and that is how he lived. Our music and creating our own music had long gone.

He came in from singing one night and said he again needed to keep half the pay as he had to go to a meeting in the morning. I had been busy staining the timber dining floor all evening but I had run out of stain and still wanted to give it another coat. I had 200,000 rupiah from selling a small item and would ask him to buy another can while he was out so I could continue while he was singing the next evening. I knew something was going on as I had found a set of vehicle keys hidden in his pocket along with another guy's car registration ID. This guy was part of his network and lived up the road. I thought it was very interesting. He had come home as usual on his bike.

Fed up with the lies and charades I thought, 'Bugger it, I am going to stick my neck out, be brave and hit this head on.' I took the keys and put them out on the coffee table while he slept. I was scared and could not go through with it, so I put them back, after photographing everything. I was angry at myself for being a coward but the fear of another beating took precedence over my wanting to expose his deceit and lies.

In the morning I asked him to pick the stain up either before or after the meeting which he agreed to do, and took the money I gave him. He then proceeded to give me this amazing account of the meeting he was going to. I stood there in astonishment as 'now' he was suddenly communicating with me but I could see through it. He was so involved in the cover-up for his real intentions that day and for the first time I saw him really struggling to not only keep his composure but his mouth had become so dry he could hardly get the words out and began swallowing deeply. Wow! Standing there, I thought he really believed I was wearing this. Meanwhile, I had papers that he needed to sign for me to go and try to renew our family card, which he had ignored for over a year and I had found out that my name should now be eligible to be on it, not just stating he was married. I plucked up the courage and said, "Oh, can you sign this please?"

I saw him study the heading but he never asked why I was doing it, as it should have been him. He just signed it and then went into the studio. He came back out with several ballad CDs in his hand. Ah, he was going to be travelling in that vehicle; as far as I knew he did not have a CD player on his motorbike and his so-called meeting was in a park. He had very little paperwork with him; another giveaway.

Off he went. The day passed and I was expecting him home so that he could go singing. The normal time had passed and I thought that he would rush in at any moment as he was late. But no, there was no sign of him and the band was now due to play. I rang the leader and asked, "Is Hass already there to play?" He said, "No, he cancelled during the week." I instantly got fire in my belly.

I turned into the gossip network during the night and learned 'they' were having a great time at the lake area they had gone to with others. Of course I heard nothing and his phone was off. He was gone the following night also and turned up at the gate at 6am on the Monday morning, of course on the motorbike. The stain I had waited for all weekend, of course, had not been purchased and I got some limp remark from him saying that he forgot to buy it. That was all I got. Once asleep

I checked and all his money was gone again, including what I had given him, and so were the car keys and registration.

A couple of people who had viewed the villa had come and gone. Things had become so tight that I had talked with Hass and told him that unfortunately I/ we would have to start selling off the band equipment which I had held off on doing for so long. I had tried to keep it so he had the total music package, not that he ever showed interest in it unless there was a reunion and he would take parts of the sound system along. It was always in the budget for expenses but if he got the money for it, he sure as hell never let on to me.

First to go were the two beautiful brand new electric guitars, bass and lead. Nothing went at once so it was a painfully arduous task of advertising, word of mouth in the musician's community, and then there were negotiations even though everything was well below half the purchase price. The property was for sale without any of the equipment, as the original plan of course was to ship it all home along with everything else, as it was still far cheaper than replacing it all later.

I forgot to mention that the week after our meeting with the woman who had loaned us the money, I had gone with Hass to pay her out and get the land certificate back. It was a shock when we went to do this as her figures were different from mine on the outstanding balance. I freaked out as it was crucial I get the certificate back. Panic had set in as I paid over what I had believed to be the final amount and due to the shortfall she and Hass suggested just having a small loan with her that did not involve her bank, but the interest was higher. I had no choice, as this was a battle I was not going to win.

These loans had been in his name as the main borrower and I was added as I was married to him, but on the second it was just his and it was put into a simple accounting book. Many people came to her for loans so she had a number of books. I had said to her or asked him to relay to her, that I could not pay the principle of this loan out until the villa was sold. I knew it was going to be a huge struggle just to meet the

interest each month. I would have to sell an item that would fetch at least this amount, if not cover the loan for a couple of months. I had the land certificate back and I had to sign off on that major loan which I made sure was also signed off in English with both our signatures. Meanwhile, daily life proceeded with lies and cover-ups for his actions. Ramadan had come around again. I struggled to make or get food for opening at sundown after a day's fasting. This humiliated me, putting me in further depths of despair. He was not home during the day but would make it in just in time to take a shower for opening time, around 6.30pm, for sholat (prayer). He would not pray with me but lie on the couch, CB in hand and pretend to sleep, and the couple of times he did, he was very bad in not leading or allowing me to hear the main prayers even though I knew them by now. I would just sit there and cry by the time sholat was completed and he would just walk away from me. Mainly though, he would leave the house again without opening with me and return just before dawn on the cusp of fasting for the day. Sometimes I was lucky and he would bring back a packet of rice for me with a small ¼ piece of chicken. I was lucky to be getting this around every 23 hours. My weight had dropped dramatically now and I looked gaunt and strained in the face. All my muscle tone was being eaten away by my body drawing on it to survive.

Whenever he did bring food home for me I was ill in the stomach every time I ate, yet if my neighbours asked me to go there to eat some food I was never sick. My dear friend, on one such occasion when I could barely eat what was offered to me, said, "You know this is Indonesia and anything can happen to you. It's best you don't eat what he brings home as you are always sick when you eat it." Then she made a bold statement which raised my eyebrows, "He is killing you softly. Be careful." She was not the only person to say this to me and she is not an over reacting emotionalist. She is a very grounded and solid Christian but she had been married to a Muslim husband and changed her religion over to Islam at that time and practiced it fully. She had suffered a similar fate that I was going through, except for the beatings.

Again I tried again to eat what was put in front of me, grateful and starving for anything to eat but the food had the same result. With any food I made, when there was some food to cook, no matter how small I was never sick! I had managed to sell the sound system but at a shockingly reduced price than what it was worth but I just had to take it. It paid the loan, the electricity, bought some food and paid some money to the credit cards. I had sent them a letter explaining my situation and they were being so patient and understanding. I just gave them reports each month.

Many locals were turning up at the gate now, including his buddies, saying they could sell the property but all wanted a hefty slug of the sale price. I had heard that anyone and everyone was a broker and to watch out for them, as they were trouble. Once I found out that they were raising my price by $50,000, so they could claim that above my price, I stopped anyone from coming. I wanted an honest sale and could not be part of cheating a buyer out of my true price.

This was one deep principle of mine; I was not prepared to compromise no matter how much I needed money. I was not popular with them or his buddies who had come with these proposals. I told Hass I would not do this and sorry, but I would not deal with anyone in this matter.

I had left all the original documents safely in the hands of a woman lawyer I had been introduced to by the first agent who just wanted to see the villa sold and me safe. Several times Hass had tried to sway me to bring the original land certificate back home but I soberly ignored this as my friends had said, 'Whatever you do, remove all the legal documents from the house and put them a safe place.' After having been robbed so easily, twice, in the past I took their advice and stuck with it.

"The best protection any woman can have is courage."

Elizabeth Cady Stanton

Broken dolls can be repaired, when you are down and out, there is only one direction to go, and that is up.

Chapter Ten

The Brink of No Return

Chapter Ten.
The Brink of No Return

After the New Year of 2011 was underway my new visa was due to be applied for where I was meant to be upgraded from KITAS to KITAP. We always started this process early as there was never a guarantee you would receive your new one before the old ran out. The system always ran behind and you would see many frustrated expats in immigration, furious and swearing extreme profanities out loud, not caring who heard them as they were aggravated by the delay.

Hass had got the paperwork and we had learned how to do it ourselves as it saved literally millions of rupiah (thousands of dollars) by not using an agent to process it all. It was fairly straight forward; just follow what you had to provide and do a simple interview.

This time it was the absolute run around. Our marriage book and certificate were no longer sufficient. We had to prove beyond doubt that we were legally married. The certificate that we needed was separate for this; it was a document of authority for permission from the Australian governor general's office to embark on a marriage. We did not have this as my old sponsor had done all the paperwork for it. I tried desperately over the coming months to get it from her but she had (let's say) gone out of business and she never answered any emails I sent, even though my server said the emails had been delivered. We explained this to the head guy we were seeing at immigration but he refused to put it through until he had sighted it. This was the same man we'd been interviewed by on every other occasion and as I said earlier, they have an amazing memory for people even after years of not seeing them.

Months were slipping past and I was getting scared because now I was in the country with no visa. We applied for a letter stating that it was in the system and processing to cover me. I applied to the governor general's office of my home country and was told it is a one off document and they do not even have copies of it. I was up 'shit creek' so to speak,

unless we could somehow get it. Hass did not seem worried about this and I wondered if this was his ploy to have me deported so that he could claim everything for him and his woman. Come hell or high water, I would fight to the end so this did not happen. I knew so many women were losing everything because their husbands had another woman.

Hass would not take me to immigration with him and always made an excuse to leave me behind or would just go and tell me later, even when the plan was for us to go together. He'd come home on such an occasion and say he had seen some guy higher up and wanted to know why this was all taking so long. The officer had told him that what was being told to us was not in fact true and my application was being processed incorrectly.

Hass said he actually saw a document where they had stated that I was to be deported. I did not know if this was an intimidation tactic of his or if this was indeed true. I had to sign another document which Hass took back to immigration the following day. I kept my fingers crossed that this time they would submit my final documents for processing. This had already taken seven months since putting in the application. It was not to be.

I wanted to go with him to find out just what was going on but he said it would be better if he went by himself. I said, "No, I am coming with you, I need to know." When I awoke the next morning, he was already gone. I was angry and frustrated. When he came back he said he had forged my signature as he forgot to get me to sign somewhere else. He explained casually that rather than travelling the fifteen minutes home to get me to sign, he went outside, forged my signature several times off the one he did have me do, and took the paper back into immigration. He showed me the rough copies of his attempt at my signature. It was very scary as he had done it so well. Now I knew I must create a new signature for myself! Good! At least he had told me what he had done for once which armed me. To him it was a little ego trip as he laughed when he showed me.

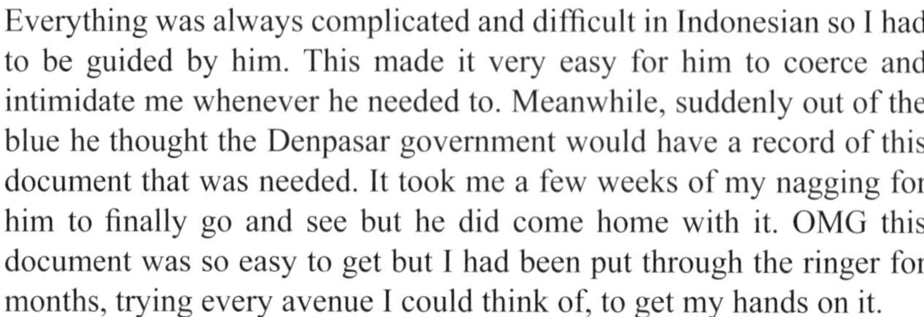

Everything was always complicated and difficult in Indonesian so I had to be guided by him. This made it very easy for him to coerce and intimidate me whenever he needed to. Meanwhile, suddenly out of the blue he thought the Denpasar government would have a record of this document that was needed. It took me a few weeks of my nagging for him to finally go and see but he did come home with it. OMG this document was so easy to get but I had been put through the ringer for months, trying every avenue I could think of, to get my hands on it.

Back he went again, returning home to say he had been advised by this guy to take the documents straight to the office in Jakarta for immediate processing. That was feasible, I thought, but now I would have to find money for the airline ticket. I was holding the money needed to process my visa as I had already sold an item. I knew that as much as I wanted to be there to witness this, there would only be money for him to, conveniently go alone as it would require a hotel room or motel. I got on the internet to find a hotel or motel close to where he had to be. Off he went. This was to be a 24 hour round trip.

He rang and said he had to stay an extra day or two for the visa to be processed. He came back with the paperwork and the contact name of the person who he dealt with. My visa would come through the mail within two weeks. He had spent all the money I gave him, which included buying new shoes, a T-shirt and other bits for himself. "Sorry," he said, "I did not buy you anything." He gave me the receipt, which was stupid of him because it was for only one night, not two and his receipt said 2 pairs of shoes but he only had one, and meal receipts for more than one person. The only thing I was interested in was getting my visa, but I wondered who got the other pair of shoes. Nothing surprised me now. I saw he had thanked a female friend and her family for their hospitality while he was there. Was there anything he did without deceit and lies? All I wanted and expected was the truth about everything.

Hass had a great time with friends who I had never stood in the way of; he had always had the freedom to do what he wanted, when he wanted as long as it did not cross the line. The only thing I had ever asked was

that he share with me as the majority of the time I was at the villa with no friends, so his outings or travels were always interesting to me. He did nothing at the villa, as it is expected that the woman (or staff, which was not our case) did the lot. A man was and is like a king as that is how they are treated from birth. Women in Indonesia are to be admired and should be the ones on pedestals and treated like queens as they work from before dawn preparing food for the day then either look after the family or business or both.

Finally, after a couple of calls to Jakarta, my KITAP visa finally came through. Thank goodness there were no more visas to process for another five years. We had to go to the central police station to register my new visa within a thirty day period so there would be no further trouble. Within a couple of weeks I received my new status from them which now was an ID card instead of this pink A4 card. It was also good for five years, until 2015.

With this out of the way it was time to seriously look for a buyer. I was sick of the kind of people that had come to look at the villa in the past 2 months. Many game players came by and I am not into games; just deal it straight and deal it fair is my motto.

The fascia on the upper level of the villa had caused ongoing problems from when it was first built. I always had to find money to fix it each time the wet season came. Those that came to fix it all had their own opinions of what was causing it and when they were paid I got the same talk over and over. It is fixed now. Oh pigs bum. It went on and on. I did other maintenance myself, staining railings, stairs, floors, re-sealed all the stone floors, did the gardens and the pool and painted the roof tiles on the garage. At least this occupied my hours in any given day.

Occasionally, I would take a stroll along the beach but a long time before that I had somewhat been put off being down there on my own because one day when I decided to go down there and fish, I had set up my rod and was ready to go to the water when I heard footsteps running behind me. This guy, a local, had his arm up in a throwing position and there was a rock in his hand. He was coming straight for me.

I was scared and made a beeline for the water. He sat waiting by the things that I had left on the sand then he stood up and started making masturbation movements with his hand at his private parts and I felt ill. There was no one around and I knew I had to get the hell out of there. I left my stuff behind and made for the track leading to my house. A local was on his way to the beach and I told him there was some crazy man who had come at me. He came with me as I went back down the beach and pointed out the guy. He informed me that he was classed as the village idiot and 'not all there.' That was the end of my attempt to fish. I would wait till I knew the locals would be going down for their late afternoon frolic in the water and sometimes brave going for a walk then. They were always friendly to me.

Hass started spending a lot of time at the beach in the heat of the day. Sometimes he would go around 8.30 or 9 in the morning and be gone for hours. I found this strange as he did not swim or sunbathe and, like most locals, avoided being in the midday sun. On a couple of occasions I went down to join him. On the first occasion he was way ahead of me and then he just seemed to vanish. I saw him, up a side street that led off from the beach, with a couple of men I didn't recognise from that distance. I just kept walking along the beach. Another time he was sitting under a little open bamboo shack on the beach. When I got there he was on his phone,

I gave him a wave and walked down the beach to where he was. He gave no invitation for me to join him and kept talking on his phone. I sat down anyway. After about five minutes of me sitting beside him he asked me to go home as a friend was supposedly coming and he wanted to finish his call. Of course the friend didn't come and the comment that he could have finished the 'chat' on the way back with me just led to a curt reply. Another time I watched him and he just sat in the same place for ages and seemed to be digging a hole in the sand with his foot. He was acting weird and looking up and down the beach every few minutes. I didn't know if he was putting something in the sand or waiting for someone but I was worried he would see me so I went back

home. His behaviour was becoming very erratic and weird. This was not the guy I had known for the past several years.

He would not answer the gate nor let me answer the gate if someone rang the bell. Sometimes, even when his friends came, he still wouldn't go to the gate, even if they called out for him. It was becoming more and more embarrassing.

My neighbour, Johanna, invited me to go with her to town one day and it was lovely to get out of the house. Of course I ran it by Hass first and he said it was good for me. This was the first time I had been out with someone, apart from my daughters, in all the years of being there. It was a real treat and I felt human again for a moment. I had no money but just to venture out with a lady friend was special for me. She bought me a loaf of bread and a bag of potatoes.

In the evenings I created special spiritual quotes with art work and would post them on Facebook. I used to get wonderful responses from people within spiritual groups who I had become online friends with and my old friends from back home. I liked to give something to make someone's day which in turn was my gift back. I also wrote poetry and song lyrics.

When In Doubt. By Sandi Allan

Life's reflection is of self, it will cast shadows,

When in doubt

Trust your instincts, as your guide

Listen, look deep inside, waiting is your truth to find.

The sun's energy gives you strength

The moon caresses, all loves intent

Shines through all, with gathered love

For your life of peace, ask you'll receive,

From heaven above.

One warm summer day I was taking it easy upstairs when I heard the gate bell ring and someone calling out. I went to the front railing on the verandah and there were a couple of Balinese men with a western guy. I guessed it was another guy scouting the area for land to buy. I guarded the gate when I opened it as people had a tendency to just walk in if it was fully open. I didn't want this as I was home alone and I was not supposed to let people in when Hass was not there, especially if I didn't know them. The guy was a big man from Australia, so that gave me a bit more comfort. The Balinese man spoke first asking, "Your place is for sale?" I reluctantly said, "Yes." Many people go round areas just asking locals for land and properties for sale. That is how I had found out about the land in the first place. I said yes it was but they had to contact the agent. I had an open arrangement with the agent, either she could sell it or I could.

The Aussie guy took over the conversation and asked if he could have a look. I tried to put him off as I had not done any special cleaning and I liked it to be well presented if someone was going to look. They pressed me until I gave in. Once he stepped in he made noises indicating that he absolutely loved the place. I had heard this many times before and just quietly allowed him to have a brief look everywhere with my guidance. He left and I thought that would be the end of it.

The next day he turned up again on his own. Hass was out again as he had gone to do his Friday sholat. This guy was very macho and I learned that he was a Vietnam veteran so I just let him be. He had brought some prawns and a beer with him. Strange and presumptuous of him but I guessed he was just being friendly. My husband came home and I told him this guy was here to see the property and that he had been here briefly the day before, with two Balinese guys. They met and he went upstairs. This guy said he was in love with the property and proceeded to go and relax by the pool and take some photos. He said he would eat his pawns and have his drink. I took some prawns up to Hass who had gone to the computer but he was asleep and ignored me when I explained that the man had brought these for us to eat and share. I was

amazed that he was asleep but also considered the fact that he could be pretending to sleep. I went and checked a couple of times but it seemed that he was. He had not touched the food.

The man left and I told Hass he seemed interested but we would wait and see. He did not respond. The next day the man came back again, very early in the morning. He had texted me to ask but as Hass was asleep in the studio I decided not to wake him to tell him, I would let him know in the morning. He was supposed to be getting up early to go out as he had started doing some work with the woman who loaned us the money, his friend. I had no Idea how much he was getting paid as he said he didn't know.

I went into the studio and woke Hass up as he was meant to be awake anyway. I told him that the man was here to see the place again as he was leaving that evening to go back to Australia and he was very keen. They actually chatted for a little while and then I said he wanted to go and see the original documents and that I would go with him. Nothing was hidden and Hass knew as much as I did. I had told the guy the price and he had negotiated with me to drop the price by $30,000 but it was still reasonable. We left at the same time that Hass left to go and do whatever it was that he was doing. I took the guy to the lawyer and he asked her to draw up the sales documents. He would send the deposit on returning home. He had already conversed with his son back in Australia and who was the executive of their business. I returned home and waited to hear from him. My lawyer gave him the bank account details where he was to deposit the money. He took a copy of everything with him for his lawyers. I was hoping this guy was the real deal and he sure made it sound that way.

Chapter Eleven

Eyes of Insanity - The Final Brutal Attack

Chapter Eleven.
Eyes of Insanity - The Final Brutal Attack

The month before, after the authorities had been to talk to Hass several times about the power bill that was overdue and which was in his name, Hass refused to go out and talk to them so they cut the power off. After he was gone I sold something and had the money to pay the bill then went with my neighbour to the government office to explain the situation in person. I asked, “If I pay now, will you put the power back on?” They said, “No, you must now pay a penalty.” I had queried what the man said when he switched the power off and he told me they wanted to take the cable too. The man in the office said, “We don’t do that.” Having been given this information my neighbour said, “Don’t pay yet, you need to hang onto that money for the moment.” I felt strange as I just wanted to pay it but as I was not thinking straight any more and I went with his decision. That turned out to be a bad move.

Hass had already gone out early while I was asleep. It was a Saturday morning. I went out onto the verandah to do something and I noticed that the black cable from the garage to the street was missing and someone had been on the verandah and cut the cable to the box. I wondered if he knew about this and had let them in to do it as the gate was padlocked. When he came home I asked, “Did you know someone has taken the electricity cable? Come and look.” He saw it and muttered that they were criminals. They had come over the wall while we were asleep and done this. I went back to the government on the Monday with my neighbour and begged them to put the power back on as they had only done this on the Saturday, but they refused. I can understand their anger because Hass refused to talk to them about it. They told me they had cancelled his account so a new account would have to be established first.

My kind neighbour then bought cable and ran a lead to the villa so that I could have a light on upstairs and downstairs. One morning when I got up Hass was in his cave in the studio and had his CB radio charging and was playing his keyboard. I said, "This cable we have from the neighbour is not for entertainment and we should not abuse his generosity so unplug those things." Where was the integrity that he always used to aspire to? This was not a game and the neighbours were not to be taken advantage of.

Hass cared about nothing but enjoying his life. Man, how he had changed from the person I had first met. I no longer understood who he was or what he was even thinking. If he wanted out he should have just said so. I had no idea why he was still living with me as he in no way acted like a husband, a friend, or the communicator which he vowed to be to others. I just wanted to scream at him but knew what would happen if I did. I was in love with this man. I had given him my heart. The only action, in silence, was that he pulled out the plugs and went to sleep until it was time for him to go out.

Here I was, having to play down and try to keep silent about having no power at the place, to any potential buyer including this man who had turned up, so that it would not turn a buyer off the property. I had bought and sold several properties so I knew the highlights and the pitfalls of sales. I did not want to lose any buyer as this meant total doom and gloom. I was feeling humiliated and a failure because of my situation. I had never had my power cut off, ever, in my life because I had not paid a bill.

Meanwhile, a couple of days later, Hass had got ready to go singing. He was about to pick up his bag with all his song books and I was about to get the key for the gate. I was standing by the chair where his books were when out of the blue he said, "How about this man?" It threw me off and I had to think who he was talking about; I may have even asked, "Who you mean?" Once I worked out who he was talking about I asked,

"What do you mean?" I thought we were finally going to have a normal conversation. Wrong!

Next he says aggressively, "And how about his heart?" "What do you mean?" I replied. "Well, you think this is a good man?" I managed to say, "Well, I don't know, I think he is okay. He is a bit of a rough cut diamond, one of the old boys, a Vietnam vet. which makes some of them a bit rough on the edge." "Oh," he says, "so long as you think he's okay." Again I replied, "What do you mean?" and he just stared at me. I'd already told Hass the man was looking at buying it for him and his Indonesian fiancé.

Suddenly I realised what he was getting at, "Oh!" I said, "Do you think there is something going on, huh? Well you're joking, I have no interest in him or any other man." He said, "How would you like it if I had a woman in the house?" What!!! I was astounded at his comments so I said, "You have been here two out of the three times he came and the first time two Balinese men came with him. Ask the bloody locals." I said "They saw me talk to them at the gate. They see everything." "Oh well," he said, "maybe I am wrong. Where did the prawns come from?" I said, "I don't know, the man brought them with him. I don't know why, just a friendly gesture, I guess." He had this weird look on his face, "What? Did you think I bought them? How would I do that with no money or transport?" I thought it was ridiculous and went to pick up the keys.

The next thing I felt the blow across my head. "What did you do that for? I have done nothing wrong except try to sell the house, which is my main interest so that we can pay the bills." Well that was it. He laid into me. Time after time, no matter where I moved to, he came after me. If I said, "Stop hitting me," I got a double dose, if I didn't say anything, I got another lot. I said, "Just go and sing." His reply as he was belting me, "And what? Not come home?" It flicked through my mind and I said, "That is up to you." I got more. I was trying to get out the door as I thought that would stop him because there were builders next door.

He is like a man possessed when he attacks you. He doesn't let up till you bleed or are crippled. His eyes were glazed and blank with vicious bitter stares as he would stalk me. If I tried to answer anything he would yell, "I told you not to talk." Whack! Countless repeated times. "I told you I count to three, if you talk after that you know what to expect." I mean, where do you go and what do you do? I have studied crisis management, yet no skills served me well nor did any good to prevent him from attacking. I need to do a course in dealing with terrifying maniacal behaviour because the system in these circumstances has no effect whatsoever.

He continued. Once he starts, you never see it coming; it was like a lightning bolt when he struck. He kept it up and said, "You older women are meant to have wisdom." Well, I had tried that too, in the past and the present, but he was like a mad-man when he started. I asked, "Why do you hit an older woman?" Stupid thing to say but when your head is getting smashed around from side to side you don't think straight. Wham! Bam! Again and again. I tried to get out onto the driveway area and yelled for help.

He came at me saying, "Are you yelling to your friends?" Whack! Nobody heard me and if the workers did, they were hiding. He continued all around the driveway. When I put my hands up and said 'stop' he smashed my wrists down with his fists which was extremely painful. I was afraid he would break my wrists and then where would I be? As he belted me again he said, "If you were a man I'd kill you right now!!!" He belted me a few more times then went and got his bag and got on his motorbike. As he rode past me he said, "And now you can go to your boyfriend." I yelled as he went out the gate that I didn't have one.

Now I knew I had to get help. Hass had threatened to kill me and he had never said anything like that before. I was a mess. My face on both sides had already started bruising up including both my eyes. I was terrified he would come home and continue it later, maybe killing me in the end. With his strength and in my physical condition, one blow the wrong way meant it was more than possible. I could not take that risk. So I locked up the house and went to my other neighbour, who had also become one of my lifesavers by giving me food. I went and knocked on the gate. I could hardly talk as my jaw was damaged. They took me in, gave me a drink and then took me to a hospital. I was x-rayed and a report was made by them for the police. We got back to the house and they came in while I quickly gathered some clothes before Hass was due home.

I went into hiding at the neighbours place until the morning. I contacted the other person who the Australian ex-detective had told me about as he was working undercover to assist westerners. He had rung me previously, after the ex-detective had told him what I was going through. My neighbours took me to him in the morning and they hid me in their car to get past my place as Hass had been texting and ringing my phone all night. I had put my phone on silent so that if he was around the area he would not hear my phone ring. I had also taken his CB radio with me.

My neighbours told their security to watch and listen but not to tell anyone I was there. They also told their day worker in the morning before we went to see my friend. His advice was to report Hass to the police this time. Prior to this, at a special meeting, he had brought in the chief of police to meet me and be made aware of my circumstances. As it turned out, he was another undercover person who I happened to know through music sources, but I didn't know he did this work. They had seen the photos of my previous beatings. I was advised to go and let the police in my area know about the situation but I had held off as some time had passed since that encounter.

My neighbours then took me to the police. I told them I had been advised to go there and I just wanted to report it, not have him arrested. This was not possible. They would not take down any details unless I made a statement. What a gruelling day. I was also afraid because of what Hass had always said about having many friends in the police force and

he could get their help to do anything at any time. I was very hesitant and had very lengthy discussions with the ever-increasing gathering of officers. I had to make a statement.

We had arrived there at about 1.30pm. I took the hospital report with me and they sat me down and I had to tell my story to them. An officer (who I thought was an officer) was translating everything I said to the one doing up the report on the computer. After I had told them everything he said, "May I take your photo? I am a reporter for a special newspaper." I was shocked. I said that I didn't want my photo taken or to end up in a newspaper. Oh God, now I had double concerns to worry about. He already had the full story and asked if I wanted Hass and his woman to be charged with polygamy and said that they would get arrested for that and put in prison. My head was hurting, my face was painfully sore and I could hardly talk. Later that day the police took me to another hospital for another report. They said I had damage to my nose, cheekbones, jaw and wrists. This was reported on a document. I was then taken back to the police headquarters. The statements continued. It was now dark. I had had no food or drink all day, not that I could eat much. They then said that I had to go upstairs to do further reports. It was a daunting place with a holding cell on the way up, containing some very undesirable people. My neighbours had gone as witness because when you file a report you must have someone who has seen you around the time of the incident, if not physically witnessed the crime in progress.

I didn't know this was happening as they were elsewhere. A tourist policeman, who was a high ranking officer, had been brought in to go through the statement with me. I said to them, "Really, I have had enough, I am exhausted." I asked, "Do I get a copy of my statement?" and he said, "No, that is not allowed." I objected to this as the statement I had to sign was only in Indonesian. He said, "I can only read out one paragraph for you, that is all you are allowed to have me translate for you." This pissed me off. He said, "You can choose which one." Well, it didn't matter a rats which one I chose as I only understood a couple of the words I could see on the screen. He said, "Trust me, it is what

you have told us." He read out the paragraph I pointed to which was accurate with what I had said.

My neighbours were going home as it was late and the police said they would take me home as they would start looking for him then in order to arrest him. Holy hell, it was on! I thought for real that they were going to bring him in after all. I was finally taken home at midnight, well, back to my neighbours. Before my neighbours or I left the police station there was a gathering in the room of the biggest men I had seen in Bali. They were not only six foot something tall but almost as broad. I thought, 'Well, if he messes with them I think he will go down in a hurry.'

To be honest, I think I had evil flickering moments of thought where I was kind of hoping these guys would get him that night, but I also hoped they didn't know him. These guys were very cool, like out there cool, and very humble towards me. I have to say without a doubt, every police officer who was involved in my case, even those from other areas who knew of my circumstances, treated me with total respect, care and concern. The tourist police officer and local officers gave great support and comfort to me. I was never asked to pay one rupiah at any stage and when I offered to give the little that was in my pocket for their social club it was immediately refused and they told me I would need the money for myself. From Kuta, Denpasar, and Gianyar the police officers on all levels were amazing. I thank them so much.

As they drove me home they observed the area. I actually thought I had seen Hass sitting up the road but as I was too scared to look intently could not tell for sure as it was a dark spot he was in and I thought it be too early for him to be back from his gig. They took me the back way into my neighbours place so that we would not drive past the front of my place. This way, if he was waiting outside, he would not see me get out of the car. I was scared stiff but these guys were very kind to me. Far different from anything I had been told about the police. Normally, apparently even for locals, if they go to the police about anything they

must pay to file a report. Not one officer asked for any money from me and when I offered to pay them, they had all refused to accept anything. People were amazed when I told them later.

The search was on for Hass. They went to the villa day and night. They had just missed him several times. He had to break into the villa as I had the keys with me. He'd sent silly intimidating texts to me trying to get a reply such as, 'Are you trying to kill the cats? They can't get outside.' I thought, 'Yes they can, the toilet and bathroom windows are open.' Even though they are small I had seen them get through the windows before, so I didn't respond. They searched for Hass for five days and I knew that he would have known as all the local security guys had CBs and he had mates all over the area with them. The police rang me after five days to ask where they could possibly pick him up. I told them that if they wanted to find him he always played at a certain place that night between certain hours. They apparently organised a plan. Two officers went and ate there, followed by two other pairs. There were a total of six officers. They watched and observed everyone who came into the restaurant as Hass had been singing there for years with the keyboard player.

Many artists from Jakarta used to go in there as well as quite a lot of westerners, even though they served traditional Indonesian food. The police apparently clapped at his singing and did what 'normal' people do. Hass thought they were from Java or Jakarta until, during the break, they got up, shook his hand and complimented his singing. Then they asked, "Are you Hass?" He replied that, yes, he was and knew straight away what was happening before they said, "You have to come with us, you are under arrest." He asked if he could do his other set. They waited then said, "You must come now." He had to go and tell the owner he had to leave and he told the keyboard player that I must have reported him for doing something wrong. The reason I and my neighbours know this is because he gave us a running report later and thought it funny how they did it and that there were six of them. They questioned him for twenty four hours. They would ask him a question, then walk out of the

room, come back and ask another. They did this for that period of time. He was asked if he wanted to go into a holding cell or sit in a chair in an office. He chose the chair of course, but that had a price.

Unbeknown to me he had bargained with them to let him out to go and do what he called his activities; his work and singing, but he had to report at 7am every morning. I had still not answered any of his text messages asking me to drop the charges otherwise he would go to prison for at least six months before going to court. I never answered because the police told me not to do anything until I heard from them. I was following their advice.

Meanwhile, the Australian was calling with all these promises of money for the villa but he had not yet sent the deposit through. Between the two things I was going nuts. By now my face was well and truly black and blue, on both sides including my chin. My right arm had a huge black bruise on the upper part and both my wrists were bruised. Two of my teeth had cracked and unfortunately pieces had fallen out on either side of my face which made it even harder to eat. My body was aching and I felt like I had been hit by a truck. Memories of my violent first marriage flooded back. I thought my life had come full circle and I was back to where I had started so many painful years before, (but that is in my second book, Stripped Back Naked, which will be released after this one). It was a very sad, heartbreaking thought.

All I could think of was what I had done wrong and question how it could happen to me again. My late husband would be turning in his grave as he hated what I'd gone through in the past. I questioned myself over and over. It is said it takes two to cause a situation like this so. I did an analysis of myself and my behaviour to find out what I had done. All I could come up with was that I avoided confrontation with him so I didn't get a beating or worse; I kept all knowledge of his adulterous indulgence to myself, never confronting him; I had copped all his lies and deceit even though it caused me to go hungry and be totally isolated from the outside world and I had sold material assets for us to survive.

I could not cook meals because there was no food or money. Yes, as a dutiful wife I had not performed well in that area for the past twelve months. I figured any reaction I did have was simply a reflection of his actions. I was not responsible for his guilt or the choices he made.

I was still staying with the neighbours as they wanted to keep me safe, even though Hass was supposedly still being held at the police headquarters. I heard talk on the CB radio saying he was there and police were making it out to be more than it was. This made me mad as they had no idea what had happened or what he had done to me, except what he was obviously feeding madam by text while being held. He was texting me and asking me to come and release him so he could get on with his activities. I ignored them all and waited for the advice of the police. After five days they rang and said I should go back up there to either have a mediation meeting with him, or proceed with charges.

I had been told by officers, which later turned out not to be the system, that it could take up to six months or longer before Hass went to court and he would have to remain in jail. The worst bit of information they gave me, which misled me in my decision to release him, was that if I sold the property I could not leave the country until it was heard by the justice department. That thought was frightening. I knew he had no intention of coming to Australia with me and I knew for my own safety that I must leave as soon as the property was sold My neighbours came with me as they too had to be involved in interviews as witnesses. I was blessed and will always be grateful that they were brave enough to assist me.

It was a room full of officers including a woman officer this time. There was Hass, me and my neighbours. They were still grilling him over what he had done to me.

In the middle of it, a plain clothes head of department entered. Hass said to me, "Oh, this is a friend from my home country, I grew up with him," and he introduced me to him. I was surprised that he found this to

be exhilarating in the middle of this serious business. It felt like it was another intimidating tactic he was using. It did not sway me nor impress me whatsoever. The officers really put it on him that his actions were totally uncalled for in assaulting me. He had completely confirmed my statement of events to be correct.

We were sent into the room next door to talk together while they interviewed and discussed the situation with my neighbours. I was nervous about sitting in an empty room with Hass but talking to him, he seemed to be totally back to his normal self and avoided discussing what had happened. It was difficult as we could hear every word being said next door and they were even discussing how we should get divorced which I felt was nobody's business but ours. I was saying this to him when he told me to hush, as he wanted to listen. He found it really amusing and was giggling at what was being said. I figured nothing had changed with him. We were then called back into the room with everyone and they asked what my feelings were about him going to court. I had weighed up everything, trying to keep all my emotions out of it and now just focused on what would be best for me. I think this would be the first time in my life that I had put me first. I had always put everyone else in my life before me. I did not value myself enough to see that I too was just as important. I said I would drop the charges against him on one condition, that he not come back to the house until I had recovered or something was sorted out between us and I wanted this in writing. They accepted this condition. It was drawn up on a legal police document saying that he was not allowed in the village where I lived or to come to the villa without ringing or texting me first to ask if he could come.

They had told him that he was not to harm me in any way or cause me any problems whatsoever. He had also been told that if he caused the police any trouble with the consulate that he would be in serious trouble. He agreed to everything and we had to sign a statement which was then signed by the police and my neighbours as witnesses. He was free to go. My neighbour suggested we take him for some lunch just to

ease the situation. That was very civilised and we just ate at a little local place. He asked if he could get some clothes so I gave him the key to go in and get some belongings. My neighbour said he could come to talk to me at their place sometimes. He had not asked me where I had been staying.

One evening he had come to my neighbours place and asked the security guy if I was staying there and said that he wanted to talk to me. The security guy told my friends and he had said he could come the next day. He rang me later that night and said he was sorry and that he still loved me. I thought, 'Don't play with my emotions any more; that can't be true,' when for a year, I had been reading the 'I love you' messages he'd been sending her. I did not give him a response and said I was hanging up. My neighbours had gone shopping when he came. I kept him outside on the verandah and their day worker was able to monitor everything. Her husband was a security guard in the local village and they all knew the conditions the police had laid down to him. He made out that he was coming to say sorry and try to get us back together but he totally blew any chance of that, no matter how slim.

I learned he had been released 24 hours after his arrest. He had negotiated with the police to let him go out to do his activities, as he called them; the small day job and his singing at night. He was secretly living at the villa which was a shock to learn. He had come to get money from me; the deal not to be put in the prison cell during the interrogation had a price, and being allowed out for his activities meant he reported to the police each morning at 7am but he told me this also had a price. He had to pay that to stay out of jail. I was horrified. He beats the shit out of me, sits there facing all my bruises without a word, an emotion or sign of remorse or face to face sincere apology and he is now asking me to pay for this without the blink of an eyelid. This made me seethe inside. I said, "I have no money; you will have to borrow it from someone else."

"Oh!" he said, "If I don't pay it they will lock me up." I had no sympathy for him I am sorry to say. I could no longer be coerced, manipulated

or intimidated. My neighbour came home and saw him there and was furious. He kicked him out. I was a bit confused at the time as I had obviously misunderstood what he had said. I was really upset at this now as I had upset my neighbour. I was going to leave but his wife talked me into staying. I sat on the bedroom floor crying my eyes out. I had given him the key to the villa to go and get more things and told him to put the key under a rock we used. I thought about that and after a couple of days took the key back as I didn't want to go to the house and find him there. He had to follow the orders.

Hass rented a room where he was working during the day and moved in. One morning my phone woke me and it was him. He had sent me a message by mistake; it was meant for his madam. It said in Indonesian, 'You awake mama honey? I go to report to the police.' She had put on her Facebook about police making a big deal of nothing. That pissed me right off but she removed the comment very quickly after someone commented back to her. I just wanted to send her the photos of my face and hear her tell me 'it was no big deal.'

After a few weeks I moved back into my place but continued to be very nervous. I had no power at the place except for the light I was getting from the line in from the neighbours. I didn't look forward to the evenings as it was very dim downstairs and so I tried to organise a light that would cover the whole area of the lounge, dining room and kitchen but would also shed a little light on the stairs. It didn't work so I used to take a torch with me when I went down to boil a bit of water. I hated cold showers so after running a lead from upstairs, down and out to the pump room to draw some water from the deep well, I would fill a large pot with water, boil it on the gas cooker and take a mini bath. This became my daily routine, just like the locals, for the next year and a half.

I could not sleep at night and would stay awake until dawn then sleep for a few hours. I'd gone from never closing my upstairs doors at night to barricading myself in. I could still hear the ocean waves with the

doors closed which was always comforting when I was trying to sleep.

I heard from the Australian buyer saying his son, being executor of his business, would not grant him permission to buy or live overseas due to his health. He had previously agreed to this but there had been trouble when this man returned home. He had offered to pay any expenses but after I informed him of the lawyer's cancellation fees, I never heard from him again. Others came and said they wanted to buy the villa but some were outright skanky and after seeking outside professional advice I cancelled one deal myself. As much as I needed a sale, the terms were hideous and put me in danger of losing everything. I had now contacted about five real estate agents trying to get the villa sold. I didn't have an exclusive listing with any of them but had a good understanding about the sale and the situation. Another guy from Australia came along and said he wanted to buy it. I had doubts about him as I listened to him discuss the price and his body language along with his eye contact was not adding up. I mentioned this to the agent.

This guy played me and the agent for a month and we both grew tired of his promises. I decided to call his bluff on the negotiations to see if he was for real, in a last bid attempt to get him to show his hand. Had he been straight up he would have got a bloody good deal and I would have lost but I was so tired of all the games, bullshit and dishonest people. Believe me when I say, while there is so much corruption, manipulating, wheeling and dealing from locals, Bali also attracts a number of expats who go there and think they can get away with anything. I had learned this from the business people I had spoken with. We still received game playing from this guy so I said to the agent, "I am done with him, don't bring him here any more. I find him insulting and he is game playing." My agent agreed with me and admitted he was also over this guy and his time-wasting ways.

I had been living on what I could buy. My wonderful neighbours had me over for meals which kept me alive. One neighbour had sold their place and moved away but still kept in contact with me. My other

dear neighbour, Johanna, said her boss needed some temporary help in the office as the manager was leaving and they didn't have anyone to replace her yet. Her boss asked if I would be interested in filling in until they had a new permanent employee; I had heard that I was now allowed to work in Indonesia with my visa as the laws had changed. I was still nervous about that as everyone you spoke to had their own slant on the new law. I was afraid and didn't want any more trouble but this was a way I could get a little bit of money to have some food and pay for a phone card and internet. She was now supplying me with a power cord. I only weighed 38 kilograms now and knew I would not be able to continue like this for long as I had been lucky not to fall ill.

I quietly took the job and used to leave home with my neighbour at 6:45 every day although I didn't start until 9am. It was my only transport. She didn't actually work in the office as she was out attending to clients all day. I would get a lift home with her around 6pm each night. It was then a matter of boiling some water for my daily cleanses and entertaining myself during the long night that followed. I had no TV, so that was out. I would do some spiritual quotes with some artwork and post them to friends on Facebook. Later, I managed to get myself the odd cheap DVD to watch. I had an understanding with the boss that if anyone needed to see the villa I would have to go home if it could not be arranged for a set time and day.

In the middle of this I had another situation. My beautiful daughter had moved to London and was to marry her wonderful English fiancée. I had said to her that if it was the last thing I would do in this life, it would be to attend her wedding. I was dying inside, knowing that unless a miracle occurred I was not going to make it to her wedding or see her walk down the aisle. This was crushing me as the time was drawing closer. We had spoken on the phone and she said it was okay and that there was plenty of time for me to meet him in the future.

One day my lovely neighbour called me to her house and said she had spoken to her boss as she had this idea and I could not miss out on

going to the wedding. Together they had worked out a plan that they would pay for my airline ticket to go and I could pay them back when I sold the property. I broke down in tears at the generosity of both of them. I did not accept it straight away as it concerned me that they were prepared to lend me this money which totally blew me away. I did a lot of soul searching and decided, after talking with them both about this amazingly generous offer of help, to accept. Now I just had to work out the how of it all as I could not leave the country without Hass's signature.

I had contact, through my other friends, with an agent who could help me. After meeting with her twice to discuss it all, I paid her the money for an exit re-entry visa but I made sure I paid enough for it to be valid for one year. I was determined I would sell the property. I actually had to sell it before April of the following year (2013) as my current driver's license had to be renewed but I could only do this by being in Australia as I had passed the period of time allowed to be able to do it through the internet.

I still had no hot water so I would wash my hair under a tap close to the deep well outside and fill my large pot to take a small daily bath. I had to juggle my two lights around at times, especially if I ran out of water at night for toilets and hand basins. I did my washing like the locals, in a bucket outside. It was only on a few occasions while working that I had enough money to buy some food to cook and eat. I was grateful for what I had and the help from my neighbours when they could give it but they all had very busy lives and were out most of the time. I lived like this from October, 2010 and it was now late in 2012. Once the villa sold, I would pay the bill and put the power back on for the new owners, at my expense of course.

I never received anything from Hass. The travel agent came back within three days with it all arranged. As I did not have his signature she apparently, as she told me, had stood guarantor for me so I could get this. I was again feeling blessed. I was afraid to leave the country even

though I had this legally stamped visa from the immigration department. My gorgeous neighbour had taken me to the hairdresser and I got my hair colour changed and it was amazing. It completely refreshed me to the point that she was astonished and said it had taken ten years off me. I looked and felt great for the first time in six years. Bless her.

I was terrified going through the airport security to leave even though I was not doing anything wrong, although I knew in the back of my mind that I was supposed to have his signature. I never did things unless it was purely the right way so anything and everything now scared me. I had no money of my own and my kind friends lent me some money so I would have something in my pocket. As I sat on the plane flying to the other side of the world, I had no idea what to expect and no money as such, I thought, 'Nobody does this.' I just followed the crowds at the stopovers and I had many layers of clothes on as I was freezing cold. I arrived at Heathrow airport where my daughter met me and I met my future son-in-law for the first time. On leaving the terminal it was a real shock to the system. I had left in 40 degree temperature to walk out into the zero degree London air. OMG!!!

My time there was wonderful, even though I froze my butt off. The wedding was absolutely beautiful and my daughter looked stunning. My other daughter also came to be chief bridesmaid. This was the first time we had been together in ten years. I was afraid all the time that I was there, thinking about my return to Bali. I was praying I would get back in without any problems. I said many prayers coming back in to land and was so relieved when I walked back out to where my neighbour was waiting for me. Praise be to God. "Thank you," I said out loud as we hugged.

In February, 2013, a lady finally showed up who was very seriously interested in buying the villa. I had spent my earnings on fixing the fascias yet again. Ramadan had come and gone and nobody had come to visit me like in the years before. I found this upsetting but accepted it. On odd occasions I was braving it to go and see a girlfriend sing in the

area where I worked. It was great to hear some music and spend some time relaxing quietly. When leaving, after the first time of viewing the property, the lady and her husband had said that they wanted to buy it. I had heard this so many times before that I just went with the flow. It wasn't long before this really was the 'real deal' and although I was afraid that it may not go the whole way, I was feeling excited that my freedom was within my grasp. It was extremely stressful indeed trying not to make any mistakes and make sure that this sale went through. I had tried to keep my personal situation out of the sale at all costs but it was revealed almost immediately. Her business manager was in the meeting with us at her lawyer's office, as was my agent.

We were about to sign the contract with pens in our hands when her business manager leaned across the lawyers desk, after she had left the room, and picked up my husband's passport. I heard him say, "I know him." With that, he immediately got on his phone and started talking to someone. I was furious at his interference and told him to stop talking to whoever it was. He said, "It's okay." I said, "No, it is not. This is a confidential deal between his boss and me." I insisted she get him to stop.

It turned out, what seemed like always, that he knew of my husband and his brothers were childhood buddies and muso's together. I now knew who he had been talking to and asking his brother to contact; my husband. I flipped. Anyway, to cut a long story short the sale was proceeding but now I had to involve Hass as, like everything else, his ID and family card had expired and for this sale to go through with him being the nominee on the land certificate all these documents must be in order or the government would decline the sale. I was really panicking and worried that I would lose this sale. I contacted him myself and asked him to come and pick up the documents from me to renew them immediately. He did this but he deliberately left my name off the family card as his wife. I had my own suspicions as to why he had done this but just sucked it up and said nothing.

It took a month of intensity, back and forth between my lawyer and hers, on a daily basis in some cases, and as their offices were at opposite ends of Bali it was no mean feat travelling between the two. Either my lawyer would not be there or hers wouldn't be available. It was frustrating to both of us. I had agreed to meet their negotiated price which meant I ended up selling the property for just the land value alone. I just wanted it to be sold and pay my debts. Hass had already signed an agreement with me, which was notarised by the lawyer, that he would not claim any of the money on the sale but I agreed to pay all debts including the ones in his name. This altogether amounted to a huge amount of $70,000. She had given me a small holding deposit while the documents on the property were finalised before she would sign the contract and pay. We had agreed to two payments to conclude the sale but by the time the contract was finally signed she was saying it could be three. I had to really stand firm and say, "Well, if you make it three then it must be completely paid for by no later than this date." It made me nervous when she kept saying 'I hope' it will be paid for by then. My agent and I were saying, "Well, now you have signed and said such and such." It was hard not to just beg for my money! She knew a little of my situation and I was hoping she would go easy on me. I trusted her but I was just so anxious, being on a deadline for going from A to B to secure my safety and plans. She was a very nice lady with good intentions and I am sure if she knew my full circumstances she would have understood why I was so nervous. If this sale had not gone through my thoughts would have been quite dark as I constantly fought the negative voices in my head, after so many promises of a sale that didn't happen.

I was not walking away with a stash of cash. I also paid back my neighbours and friends for all their help with electricity, financial loans and incidentals which I was only too happy to return. More than anything, I needed to try to pay everyone back for all the generosity and help they had given me over this long period of time. I wanted to walk away with a clean slate.

I had debts that needed to be paid which amounted to a considerable sum and which I wanted to get paid as soon as I possibly could. Everyone, both in business and privately, had waited with enormous patience and trusted me completely. I am indebted to them all for their amazing trust in me. I can never thank my family, friends and creditors enough. I did not have a list a mile long but I believe in honesty, integrity and honouring one's debts.

Words of Hope

(originally written by Pearl Buck 1892-1975)

There are many ways of
breaking a heart

Stories are full of hearts
broken by love,

But what really breaks a heart

Is taking away its dream

Whatever that dream may be.

Chapter Twelve

The Contract - The Taste of Freedom

Chapter Twelve. The Contract - The Taste of Freedom

I felt like everything was so close yet still so far away. The buyer had still not signed the contract which was making me feel ill to the very pit of my stomach. Anything could happen and I was in the hands of the almighty. I was praying night and day that he would release me from this hell.

There was confusion over this document and that document and it was really testing all the strength and courage of my patience and belief in this sale being successful. My agent was also on tenterhooks as we went back and forth to get the documents correct and in order. My lawyer had told me that in the past with pending sales, everything was in order for a sale to proceed but when it came to the crunch this was not the case. I had to work hard on pushing down my frustration, but realised that had one of the previous buyers been the real deal there would have been a lot of problems in getting a sale through. My confidence in her was truly being tested by the day as my buyer's lawyer really dotted the I's and crossed the T's, which was refreshing.

I could see now why there was always much talk about lawyers and how they performed their duties. At one point, under the guidance of my agent, we actually sought the advice of an independent authority just to have her slant on this deal. She informed us that there shouldn't be such delays and said that I should question them on what they were doing. It was all becoming too much for me mentally and emotionally. I was in everyone else's hands and had little control over what was happening any more. Where I had stood my ground early in the process I was now being overridden by the buyer and her lawyer. I understood where the buyer was coming from and in all fairness, totally understood, but she was really putting me through the wringer. She was a very successful Indonesian business woman. She was buying the property for her son

and his wife to live in and wanted to get in as soon as possible to do renovations at the villa to suit her style.

She had stipulated that she wanted to meet my husband so I had to arrange this at my lawyer's office. She would not buy the property unless she met him. It was here that I had been told by my lawyer, prior to the meeting, that I was not to say anything and had to keep my mouth shut. I learned in this meeting that if a few things were not set out a certain way I would never be able to sell the property and that the property would be taken by the government. This was the first time I had heard anything like this. She had never once given me any indication that these were the facts in the situation. So, with all the past potential buyers I had taken there, I was being led up the garden path. This was an astounding revelation to me. I sat there while she read out the complete sales contract in Indonesian to my husband and the buyers. He agreed with everything and so did they. After that, we made a mad dash to her lawyer, which in the traffic was an intensely abnormal hour and half drive. I was with the buyers in their car. My husband did not have to attend so we departed after a few words.

I now knew that all I had heard and all the newspaper reports about land deals going wrong for expats were in fact the truth. I had been set up from the start and now the text message I'd received out of the blue from my first lawyer, a year after buying the property, made sense. He was apologising to me for all his unprofessional conduct!!! That was a mild statement. Finally she signed and the deal was on. Up to this point anything could have happened. I now had to organise myself. I was excited but at the same time very nervous of my own situation.

The buyer was supposed to send the money directly to my Australian account. My husband had known this from the very outset when the plans were for us to sell and go to Australia when it was sold. She went back on her word with many reasons why she and her lawyer could not do this. I was forced to open up an account locally and then do the transfer myself. My agent and I had worked out why they would not do

the transfer as per our agreement. I was gravely concerned while the money sat in an account in my name in Bali and discussed it with the wonderful service person at the bank when I had to make the transfers. I lost large amounts of money having to do this.

The second payment was to be at the end of March, the following month, so I started packing up all my belongings. I had given my husband all his belongings months before, including some of our accumulated furniture and extra comforts. I was sad that I had had to sell the keyboard as the very last item. I had desperately tried not to sell it as I wanted to give it to him, but only a couple of months before, I had to pay for the failing fascias which had collapsed yet again, leaving gaping holes in several places. If the place was ever to get sold I had to make the decision to repair the damage caused by the rain.

I stored what I could physically move on my own in the studio so that when I did bring in the cargo guys it would be quick and easy for them. I also had to arrange to get my teeth fixed before leaving as it was so expensive to get the work done back home. I had not been to a dentist for six years so apart from my broken teeth I knew there would be some other work that needed doing.

I had to be ready when the third payment was paid. With the first deposit I had paid off the loan for the villa. On depositing it in the woman's account and telling her this account was now cleared of any debt owing, I learned that yet again she wanted more. According to the agreement Hass and I had after he had come and got the monthly payment from me a week after the beating, while I was staying at the neighbours, I said, "I am not paying this any more. Now you have the responsibility," and he agreed with me. I had even sent her a text message to this effect while he was standing there.

Once he knew the sale was going through he was quick to say his friend was asking about the loan money. I said I had not received any payment yet and she would get it when I had. I honoured this.

Anyway, he had not paid any of it in sixteen months. She apologised in a return message to me and said he had not told her about this. I was furious with him as he had been earning money all this time, not only from her but also from his singing. He had never asked how I was, let alone offer 1 rupiah to help me. I guess I knew where and what he was spending his good income on! I paid her straight away and figured that was the end.

I was afraid at the villa as I never knew what could happen and just proceeded with my plan. It had to go like clockwork. I went to the dentist, thinking the black bits that had appeared around my gums and teeth were because of my lack of nutrition. As it turned out, they were all cavities. They had never given me trouble so I was totally unaware of this. In the end I had nineteen cavities filled (shocking) and my two broken teeth fixed. I didn't mind smiling again with my new, clean, healthy teeth. Now I just had to learn to use them again. It was painful for me to eat as my jaw had never been realigned after the beatings.

My agent had put me onto a cargo company and I had them come to assess the cargo I was taking back to Australia. I figured I owned it and it would be cheaper than replacing it on arrival in Australia and weighing up the cost, I saw I would still be ahead. They could not do the packing when I needed it as many ceremonies had also come around. This worried me as the longer it was delayed the longer I had to wait to make my arrangements for leaving.

I had taken a weekend out to spend with my dear singer girlfriend. She sang with a mature musician who, at one stage after my last beating, had felt something was wrong as I never came to listen to them with Hass any more. When he arrived that day he said he had asked Hass where I was and Hass had said he had a problem with me. This muso said to me, "If Hass had a problem with me, then I would not have caused it," and he came to see for himself. He was shocked to learn what had happened. He and his brother, who came with him, very generously left me with some money which I had never expected. I

went and gave it back to him one night with my singer girlfriend as they were performing together.

He did not want to take it back but I insisted and got her to translate and say how grateful I was for his concern and wonderful help. He told me I must now just look after myself. I took her on a treat for the weekend and we had fun together just hanging out, listening to music, singing and dancing and relaxing as she always gave to her family and never had the opportunity just to enjoy her life.

The buyer was about to make the final payment and the cargo company had only just started to do the packing. I thought they would be like the Australian guys who packed every item from the house, barn and office into my container to be shipped; they arrive one day at 7.30am and shut the door of the container at 4.30pm of the same day. Huh! This is not the case in Bali. They come at 10am look at every item and then pack it. Not one day but five in total! I was freaking out. All the locals were observing everything and I was concerned about word getting to Hass that I was on the move.

On the final day of packing the buyer made the last payment. I left the packers to it with my neighbours staff watching over the villa. I rushed into town, made the final payment and went to the ticket office and purchased my aeroplane ticket. It was Friday so I was highly stressed and extremely nervous. I left there and went and booked myself into a quiet resort from that night until I left. After doing these things I returned to the property and the workers were putting the last few things on the truck.

The new owners arrived, with the business manager, at 6pm to get the keys to the place. She had already organised for her building team to start renovations in the morning. She too was not wasting any time. This made me very nervous as the manager could blow the whole thing for me. I had already warned him that he was not to pass on any information after the altercation at the lawyer's office and warned him that I would find out. It had come to pass before when I had been aggressively approached by Hass after that time when he found out this guy had been to the property. I let the guy know that the only other time he had come with the buyers I had been questioned by Hass, so he knew my words were truth and not drama.

When they were leaving I was asked where I was moving to and with the guy in the driver's seat hanging on every word we spoke, I just said I was moving into town. She pushed for further information so I'd said the Renon area which was in close proximity to where I was going to stay. I did not like to tell her a lie but I needed to protect myself.

I was so close to freedom I could almost taste it and I was not going to let anything get in my way. There were only four people who knew my exact plans and where I was going to be. These were the only ones I could completely trust. I had dinner with my beautiful friend and neighbour and days spent with my other friend. I tidied up the few last things that needed doing. Monday came around. I went to the cargo company and paid the money for shipping then I went to the hairdresser and got my hair refreshed for my flight home.

On Monday evening I had dinner with my agent but stayed within the safety of the resort. I could not sleep at all that night. I had gone to sit on a chair and missed it, falling to the floor and hurting my back and arm. I thought, 'This is all I need. Be careful girl, you don't need any broken bones now.' I guess the mental weight I was carrying had just got too much. My family knew my plans and were beside themselves with excitement for me. I had one last situation during the nice dinner with my agent when a friend had pushed me by phone the previous night to give some assistance. He sent a messenger to pick up the money from me, which he did in front of my agent at the table. I had him sign a receipt on behalf of this guy who made pleas and promises! I'm still waiting for it to be honoured even though many months have passed yet again! I gave him the trust he asked for as my final one in the land of the Gods, sad to say. I came in trusting and left doing the same thing. I have finally got it. The lesson!

My girlfriend was coming early in the morning. This was my big day. My freedom was just a matter of hours away now and I waited for my friend as there was no way she was not coming to the airport with me as sad as she was to be saying goodbye. We shared some food on arrival at the airport, chatted and took photos. She had brought me a gorgeous little bouquet of my favourite flowers. When it was time to leave I said, "Darling, I have to give you the flowers back now as I cannot take them with me or they will be destroyed at the Australian airport." I wanted nothing to prevent me from clearing customs quickly. "Take them home and know I am beside you."

She cried as we hugged and said our goodbyes. I was overloaded with baggage and planned on paying for my excess of one case. On presenting my passport and ticket to security, one officer looked at my three cases and said, "What? Just one person?" I inwardly panicked thinking, 'Please don't stop me now.' I still had my exit re-entry visa which was good until December, 2013. This particular visa allowed me or the holder of this type of visa to come in and out of Indonesia several times throughout its term without having to report or make further applications or payment to immigration. I had replied, "Yes," and moved towards the security scanning area for the luggage. I could not take the trolley any further and it was extremely awkward trying to manage my cases. He finally assisted me which was a blessing.

Feeling nervous and overwhelmed after going through and clearing the scanner, once again I could not manage my luggage. I was really stressing as I did not want to draw any attention to myself but I was doing just that. I was tripping over my bags trying to organise them to roll as I walked. Yes, you could say that I was paranoid and you would be right. Finally, a guy indicated there were trolleys ahead of me which I had not even seen due to my stress levels. I made my way to the check-in counter. All went well and they did not charge me for my luggage, the reason being that as their direct flights were entirely booked out for the next three weeks, I'd had to take a business class ticket. Although this was double the price, to me this was not about money but about my

freedom. I had not flown business class since being in the film and TV industry and forgot the attention and service that came with it. I was blown away at being so well looked after and totally spoiled by the Virgin flight attendants. It was very fitting as my daughter in England was a flight attendant with them before embarking on her new journey in life with her husband. I was so thankful that the angels were shining down on me. I remembered thinking to myself, 'God has granted me my freedom and I am so thankful and blessed.' I now prayed that there would be no problem returning to my beloved Australia. As a permanent resident I had not been able to get back home since 2005 and literally prayed during the flight that there wouldn't be any problems. I was over my limit on a few things but declared everything completely. I figured that if I had to pay for something, then so be it. It was the longest five hours of my life.

I told the officers what I had when asked and was ushered to a particular area. I waited for a customs officer to see to me. He too asked what I had and as they had an investigation going on he said, "Off you go." Oh what a gift to receive, "Thank you very much," I replied. I pushed my trolley towards the doors with an overwhelming sense of excitement running through my whole body. Three more steps to take. The doors opened and I was greeted by my daughter, son in-law and a bigger surprise, my granddaughter who I had not seen for ten years. She had grown from a little girl into a beautiful young woman.

It was a weird feeling realising that it was finally over. It had taken three years of patience, pain, grit and guts to finally be standing safely on Aussie soil again. Oh! The absolute exhilaration. I leaped in the air and let out a squeal of delight saying, "I am home! Yippee!" Thank goodness there weren't too many people out there but I didn't care. I really wanted to scream with joy and run up and down the terminal while doing it. It was all so surreal. I said a quiet prayer of thanks while travelling in the car with my family.

I am still coping with trying to let go of my fears, which are still very much a part of me and taunt me on a daily basis. It is going to take time to adjust to normal life and society again where I am able to feel and show my emotions and express them. Just getting back into talking again and having a normal conversation after being isolated for so long is taking time. My confidence and self esteem which had been stripped away will grow again as I settle back in. I have to learn how to eat again as my teeth and jaw still ache when I eat anything. I have trouble digesting food but this will correct itself over time. I take a long time to eat a standard meal (yes, to all my friends who know me, be warned, I take even longer now, ha, ha) and I am sure I bore people nearly to death while they wait for me to finish, but they are kind and patient. Sometimes I just stop eating because I feel embarrassed.

The worst part is that now I have a form of agoraphobia. I have to really push myself to go out even though I enjoy the freedom, atmosphere, beautiful scenery and interesting people everywhere. I am also still afraid to contact old friends on the phone to chat. As much as a part of me wants to, I find the chatter in my head talks me out of it. It is strange but I now find the nights very lonely by myself, even though I have been on my own for so long. I think it is because now that I have access to places and am able to go out, join with people, laugh and enjoy simple pleasures at the same time it is very scary for me. I cry at any sad event on television; I cry waiting to go to sleep at night.

I have to give myself permission daily, to not only feel free but to be free. Yes, legally, in Indonesia I am still married to Hass and I am, according to my visa, supposed to return. Legally, the only way to divorce is to go before an Imam of the government judge of Islam, (an easy way to explain it) in Bali with him and put the case before him. He decides whether the divorce will be granted or not. He then takes back the original marriage certificate, which I have, and gives a legal document of divorce if he grants it. Yes, it is written in the holy Quran that a man can divorce his wife by saying, "I Divorce You" three times in three consecutive months, but as Hass never said those words

at any time that makes it irrelevant in our circumstances, but still, to make if officially legal one must go before the judge, as I mentioned. A woman can divorce her Muslim husband on the grounds of abuse. All the pain and neglect is still very much alive within me and until I seek counselling to overcome the grief of what I have endured, I will not be whole again. I am crushed and heartbroken by what has happened and this will take time to heal. You can't keep a good woman down for long and I am making roads back to a successful and happy life.

I was sad not to be able to say goodbye to the other family members that stood by me and helped me in adversity, which was breaking tradition, but I will always feel honoured and very thankful that they were willing to come to my aid and support me.

Compassion is the basis of morality and integrity. It is not about what country you live in, or the culture, nor is it about religion. It is individually shown from one person to another. Many people have asked me, "Do you still love him?" I would be lying if I said, 'No, I don't.' In any relationship there are memories of great and good times as well as the bad and evil. I do miss those great times, as they were not a lie from my side!

I cannot blame him, or despise him for what he did, he just never got it, as that is how he is and chooses to be in 'his' life. I am able to forgive, but this does not mean I forgive, excuse or forget the acts of violence and abuse I received, the lying, infidelity and total betrayal in so many ways. I thank him for the lessons I have learned which enable me to continually grow as a person.

I will pick up the pieces and although I failed to do good over there, I am sure I can help some people at home or elsewhere, knowing that if you keep going and hold onto your beliefs that they can get you through the troubles. I did not survive this for no reason. I must turn it around and find my purpose in being here. We are not given repeated chances for nothing and that is why I have committed to relevant extensive studies in counselling, to assist those in need.

Many women, even here, are experiencing a similar fate as I but from the reverse side. Their husbands have left them and their children to chase the ever-increasing fascination of the Indonesian and Asian women and what they think is an easy and exciting lifestyle in Bali. Every time I hear their true story from older and younger women my heart goes out to them and their children. I want to cry for them. They are hurting, disillusioned and heartbroken.

I have witnessed young and old men in Bali, crying into their beers after they have given everything to their new-found loves only to be left with empty pockets and broken hearts and dreams. The bars are full of them, night and day. Many couples go there to enjoy life together only to find within a very short time that their solid marriage is over. On most of these occasions, the man has found himself a lover. I am very happy for those western ladies who have married Indonesian men and who seem to have a successful marriage but some of them have had to give up their homeland citizenship so that if something goes wrong and they split up they don't lose their children to the husband's family. This is very sad that they have had to do this and I know of several that, in fact, have had to do so.

Meanwhile, I will build another dream to work towards. I will continue to write my songs and hope one day that I can record and release them with an artist again. I hope I can find a female artist with a great Blues voice who will be willing and find my 'Mamas Heart' worthwhile recording.

My life is far from over unless the almighty decides otherwise,

I remind myself,

"Let Me Remember. Intent is always revealed in the outcome. No one else is responsible for what I want. My blessings have my name on them. I can only have what is mine by Divine Right. I cannot lose. Lack of honesty always reaps a lack of satisfaction."

(Quote by Iyanla Vanzant)

The Ugly Truth We Try To Hide From

Life is the good, the bad and the ugly.
It's laughter, loneliness, pain, sorrow, fear,
Courage, strength, joy, truth, realisation.
Honesty smacks you in the face when you least expect it,
Don't run and hide from it
If you see it, admit it, acknowledge it
Sit in it
It enlightens you, it releases you
You will be set free.

By Sandi Allan

I don't have money or power. I am an ordinary person with no great abilities. I have simple thoughts and do simple deeds. In the past, for as long as I can remember, I have always said, 'It's okay, it will be alright, it will change.' I have finally come to realise this is not the case. For change to occur one must be brave and step forward and step up even though you have fear and trepidation of the outcome.

What I do have and recognise, which I need to honour, is the gift that I have been given from the almighty. This is a blessing of inner strength. This is my salvation from whatever life delivers me.

Even though I believe I have always been my own person since a child, but in a timid way, it felt like I have always been like a 'genie in a bottle' that could never get out. There was always something stopping me or holding me back. These past ten years, I again became that genie in the bottle, only this time the lid had been forced shut. Now I am out I will never be put back or return to the glass cage. I have broken free.

As much as I am sitting here in fear of writing and telling my story to you, I feel obligated to stand up and acknowledge the many thousands of women around the world who are abused and violently violated by their husbands, partners or strangers. They live their life in fear and in silence for various reasons. It is through fear for their life, fear of being outcast, fear of being alone, fear of intimidation, being reduced into submission and afraid for their children.

I have decided, after years of abuse in my life one way or another, that I cannot allow my soul and psyche to be destroyed any further. I must claim back what is rightfully mine.

I choose to be a voice on behalf of all women around the world who are in pain and suffering from abuse, violence and other atrocities inflicted upon them. I have been silent long enough.

The saying that I was given so many years ago, when I no longer wanted to be abused was, 'You made your bed, now lie in it.' This went out in the sixties and seventies. We no longer have to endure or face this alone. This is not acceptable nor should any woman have to accept this to make others feel comfortable or so they can pretend this is not occurring. No woman gives her permission to be violated in any way.

There was no closure between us therefore sadly, as I close my book, I realise this may be the only closure I will ever receive. I am surrounded by my loving family and dearest friends. I will be okay.

Empowered Verse To Honour All Women

Women are so scared and deserve to be honoured, treated with respect and dignity.

They are the life force of our universe, our world.

They are the nurturers of mankind.

They are the voice of the unborn child, their eyes, their smiles, their tears, their pain.

They are the strength, the courage, the love of humanity,

They are the Angles of Eden's Earth.

By Sandi Allan

If only one person reads my story and I am able to give them some hope, then everything has been worthwhile. If am able to, I want to remind them that they have a voice, the strength and courage within them to believe in themselves.

There is always a light at the end of the tunnel. No matter what someone may have to dig through, don't give up. It only takes one step at a time to free oneself from incarceration.

I send out my prayers and blessings to you. Know that no matter where you are, no matter what you do, no matter your circumstances, you are not alone and the universe loves you. God bless you and keep you safe from all harm.

It isn't for the moment

You are struck that you need courage,

But for the long uphill climb back to sanity.

By Anne Morrow Lindbergh, b. 1906

My Quote for today...

Life is the candle that never burns out,
Life is the energy when you are in doubt,
Life lifts you up when you're falling down.
Life is in the air, in the ocean depths below,
Life follows you, wherever you may go.
Life is in the North, South, East and West,
Life never sleeps, it continues to caress
Life blesses you, while you silently lie to rest.

by Sandi Allan

Thank you for sharing my story, May your life be filled with joyous celebration.

Blessings from the sky.

Author's final words in dedication to all abused and violated women around the world.

It is difficult to let go of something that has become so familiar to you, someone who you know but no longer provides you with love and honesty. In your heart you know it's at the end. It is essential that you release the part of yourself that is attached, in order for you to honour yourself and to live a life without abuse and violence. Surrender. Let go gracefully and trust in yourself.

The reason why most women lose their beauty and fade is due to psychological damage from abuse. Lack of true love inflicts terrible emotional damage on a woman. Her eyes are the soul of love. The eye assumes a totally different form in the presence of love. One's voice becomes totally diverse. The voice of someone who loves is very different from that of someone who does not. Love makes a woman beautiful; it beautifies her passion and zest for a fulfilling life. But women collapse unbelievably quickly when it is absent. The heart cannot be fooled.

I see it sometimes. Many pretend to be laughing and joyful, as I did to cover my pain and sorrow. They seem to smile, but how embarrassing and degrading it is to do that and play such games for the sake of money and false love. Since it is near impossible to deceive someone who knows they are not really loved, it means a lifetime of sorrow. That precious quality in their souls disappears, or is wasted and that is terrible dishonour to one's soul.

An example of pretentious love; A man or women first begins feeling a powerful love when they first see a new house they want to have, don't they? If the house is a very expensive one, they begin feeling a very powerful need. They will do anything to get it, It is the same as if a person is perceived to be rich, then that conceited love dazzles the predator and they become ready to do anything. Later, once the

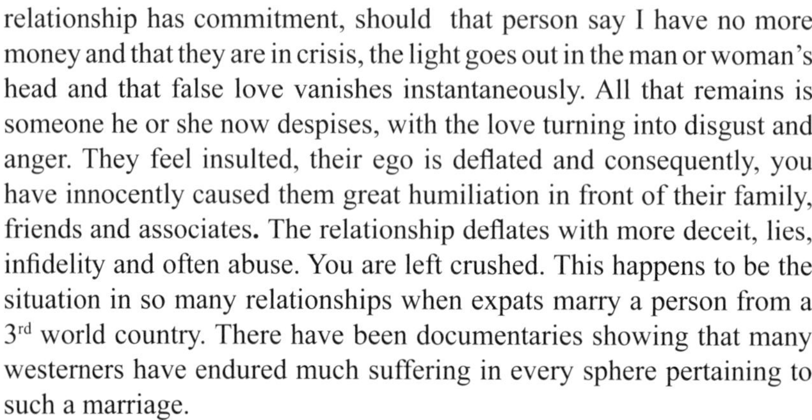

relationship has commitment, should that person say I have no more money and that they are in crisis, the light goes out in the man or woman's head and that false love vanishes instantaneously. All that remains is someone he or she now despises, with the love turning into disgust and anger. They feel insulted, their ego is deflated and consequently, you have innocently caused them great humiliation in front of their family, friends and associates. The relationship deflates with more deceit, lies, infidelity and often abuse. You are left crushed. This happens to be the situation in so many relationships when expats marry a person from a 3rd world country. There have been documentaries showing that many westerners have endured much suffering in every sphere pertaining to such a marriage.

At the heart of honest love lies, of course, honesty, loyalty and trust. One receives an uncontrollable delight when this is true love and it is open to see. In the absence of these, neither men nor women have any power to love and that's when the games come to the table and impersonations begin. Two stage actors begin their wearisome and difficult acts and impersonations intended to deceive the other person, sometimes for the rest of their lives. False laughter, speech, compliments and love enters the equation; it is torture. A secret loathing develops. One will appear to love although actually does not. If you have knowingly lied about your love for the person you have married, it is only a matter of time before you are exposed. Nothing survives on lies, deceit, abuse and violence.

" A lack of transparency results in distrust and a deep sense of insecurity."

Dalai Lama

Recommended Resources

National Sexual Assault, Family & Domestic Violence Counselling Line **1800 737 732**

- LifeLine
- Translating & interpreting
- Kids Help Line
- Australian Childhood Foundation
- Relationships Australia
- Our Place Online

- LifeLine
- For telephone counseling (general)
- Ph. 131 114

- Kids Help Line
- Telephone counseling for children and young people

Free Call to Australian Childhood Foundation Counselling for children and young people affected by abuse in Australia.

Ph 1800 176 453 or (03) 9874 3922.

- Freecall: 1800 551 800.

Other Book References

INFIDEL my life by International Bestseller Author AYAAN HIRSI ALI

What Husbands Wish Their Wives Knew About Men Best Selling Author Patrick M Morley

The Reality Slap International Best Selling Author Dr. Russ Harris

You Can Heal Your Life Author Louise L. Hay

Sex Drugs and Meditation Author Mary-Lou Stephens

Happiness Is Just a Breath Away Author Kawena (Gwen Gordon)

Unlocking The Secrets to Longevity, handing you the key Author Sonia Crystella

101 Ways to Win a Woman's Heart Author Jane Roder

About the Author

Sandi Allan

Poet, Songwriter, Artist, Television & Film Production Manager, 2nd Assistant Director, Script Supervisor, Location Manager.

Always ambitious, Sandi landed her first job when she was only 10-years-old. Using her wits, she started upon a career path that reflected her love for caring for people.

After working as a nurse's aide in a home for the aged, Sandi a school gymnastic champion and national level qualified gymnastic instructor opened a gymnastic club. She trained girls in the Hydro Scheme Government Village. With her guidance, all girls were awarded their iron and bronze medals at the one time, which was a very rare achievement. Her success was rewarded with the New Zealand Gymnastics Association National Levels Examiners qualification.

Sandi was then asked to train a high school girl's gymnastic team, which she did totally on a volunteer basis of no monetary gain to her. Her reward was in the results. She drove them including their sports teacher through icy roads one hundred and thirty miles to compete. Although the team had never participated in the South Canterbury Inter-Schools Gymnastics Championship, it was Sandi's coaching that led them to victory. It was one of the proudest moments in her life.

Soon, after moving with her family to Queensland Australia in 1979, Sandi's career turned towards television and film. After a period of time being in front of the camera in small roles she built a casting agency, for actors and entertainers before becoming more involved in television and film production. Many years later while working as assistant location manager during the filming of Paperback Hero was working with the incredibly down to earth Hugh Jackman, producers and film crew.

Her love for helping others led to working with homeless and at-risk youth from all parts of Australia. She lived alongside them in the bush in South East Queensland and taught them survival skills. This experience was extremely rewarding and satisfying part of her life as a mentor and life coach. This she did with her late husband as committed members of organisations in quiet times of the film industry.

Sandi went on to work on hundreds of television commercials. Her contribution to the television industry includes work with Roly Poly Picture Company, Granada Television in the U.K. and Canada, Young & Rubicon in the USA, Warner Brothers Movie Studios in the Gold Coast, United Film & Television Broadcasting U.K. & The Australian Film Co.

Sandi was made a life time member of the Wasp Creek Rural Volunteer Fire Service and it was her compassion for people that motivated Sandi to produce a special-effects narrated version of her poem "Heroes of the Bush." She dedicated the moving poem to the Wasp Creek Firefighters of Queensland and all volunteer firefighters throughout Australia. The poem is played on every Australia Day.

In addition to poetry, Sandi loves music, songwriting, and singing. She enjoys singing a song she wrote entitled "Mama's Heart." She wrote the song not only to share with her own children, but to also share with mothers throughout the world.

While living in Bali, Sandi wrote and produced a special effects version of a song dedicated to the victims of the Tsunami that struck in Aceh, Indonesia in 2004 and all suffers from all the countries . T'sunami Hearts the Weep has been professionally recorded nut her financial situation stopped her chance to release it,but she still hopes to release it one day and to record her "Mama's Heart".

Unfortunately, life has dealt Sandi a series of devastating blows. This is revealed in her following book ' Stripped Back Naked',

Ever resilient, Sandi is now studying at the Australian Institute of Professional Counselling to obtain her counseling diploma in several fields to perform locum work assisting the less fortunate once her studies are completed. Her life's mission is to be a spokes person, life coach and advocate against abuse and violence against women and children.

Sandi lives in Queensland, Australia.

Making Violence against Women Count

Facts and Figures - a Summary

Press release, 05/03/2004

The following statistics outline the gravity and magnitude of the problem of violence against women throughout the world. However, such figures do not show the true extent of this human rights violation. They cannot be comprehensive or exhaustive and must therefore be interpreted with caution. There is a lack of systematic research and statistics on violence against women. Many women do not report it - they are ashamed or fear skepticism, disbelief or further violence. The fact that there is no information on this problem in some countries and extensive information in others does not mean that the problem is country specific. On the contrary, it emphasises the need for more research, so that it can be studied and tackled.

Hakimi M, Nur Hayati E, Ellsberg M, Winkvist A.
Silence for the Sake of Harmony: Domestic

Violence and Health in Central Java, Indonesia.
Yogyakarta, Indonesia: Gadjah Mada University;

The same techniques were applied to the likelihood of a woman leaving an abusive relationship and it was found that 70 percent of women eventually did leave their abusers, although some women stayed as long as 25 years or more before separating. Stratifying this analysis according to age groups shows that younger women are more likely to have left an abusive relationship within four years, compared to women between 35-49 years (Figure 12.13). This indicates that younger women are less likely to tolerate abuse than older women.

Introduction

Violence against women is an obstacle to the achievement of the objectives of equality, development and peace. It both violates and impairs or nullifies the enjoyment by women of their human rights and fundamental freedoms. In all societies, to a greater or lesser degree, women and girls are subjected to physical, sexual and psychological abuse which cuts across lines of income, class and culture. The low social and economic status of women can be both a cause and a consequence of this violence.

1

Violence against women throughout their life cycle is a manifestation of the historically unequal power relations between women and men. It is perpetuated by traditional and customary practices that accord women lower status in the family, work place, community and society and it is exacerbated by social pressures. These include the shame surrounding and hence difficulty of denouncing certain acts against women; women's lack of access to legal information, aid or protection; a dearth of laws that effectively prohibit violence against women; inadequate efforts on the part of the public.

1

United Nations, 2005.

Chapter 6

Violence against women

Key findings

- Violence against women is a universal phenomenon.
- Women are subjected to different forms of violence – physical, sexual, psychological and economic

– both within and outside their homes.

- Rates of women experiencing physical violence at least once in their lifetime vary from several percent to over 59 percent depending on where they live.
- Current statistical measurements of violence against women provide a limited source of information and statistical definitions and classifications require more work and harmonisation at an international level.
- Female genital mutilation – the most harmful mass perpetuation of violence against women – shows a slight decline.
- In many regions of the world, longstanding customs put considerable pressure on women to accept abuse; authorities to promote awareness of and enforce existing laws; and the absence of educational and other means to address the causes and consequences of violence. Images in the media of violence against women – especially those that depict rape, sexual slavery or the use of women and girls as sex objects, including pornography – are factors contributing to the continued prevalence of such violence, adversely influencing the community at large, in particular children and young people.

2

The Beijing Platform for Action requested all governments and the United Nations, among others, to promote research, collect data and compile statistics relating to the prevalence of different forms of violence against women (especially domestic violence) and to encourage research into their causes, nature, seriousness and consequences as well as the effectiveness of measures implemented to prevent and redress violence against women.

3 An elaboration of the situation with regard to statistics on violence against women was presented in the previous issue of *The World's Women.*

4

2 Ibid.

3 Ibid.

4 United Nations, 2006a.

Wife-beating is a clear expression of male dominance; it is both a cause and consequence of women's serious disadvantage and unequal position compared to men. Indicators related to perceptions of wife-beating aim to test women's attitudes towards gender roles and gender equality. In many regions of the world, women are still expected to endure being beaten based on ingrained social conditioning about the status of a wife. The strength and weight of traditions is such that many women even find it justifiable to be physically punished in certain circumstances. The series of Demographic and Health Surveys conducted in countries and regions all over the world included questions regarding women's attitudes towards violence they suffered or were expected to suffer as a consequence of their acts and behaviours. Specifically, questions asked whether a husband was justified in hitting or beating his wife if she burnt the food, argued with him, refused to have sex with him, went out without telling him or neglected the children.

It has to be emphasised that not all women in these societies and countries have the same level of acceptance of physical punishment. Education certainly plays a crucial role in rejecting these "entitlements to violence" bestowed on husbands.

Indonesian women struggle against poverty, discrimination and exploitation By Zely Ariane, in Jakarta

International Women's Day is still much less known among Indonesian women than May Day is among Indonesian workers. This is not surprising because the struggle for the liberation of women developed only several years after *reformasi* - the movement that toppled the Suharto dictatorship in 1998. Then there was a mushrooming of different kinds of women's organisations, communities, non-government organisations (NGOs), research institutions and legal aid that openly advocated women's social and political rights.

Before *reformasi,* for 33 years the Indonesian people lived under the dictatorship of Suharto, who politically and organisationally suppressed the ideas of women's liberation and equality. Not killing only ideas, the regime also killed or imprisoned thousands of activists from the Indonesian Women's Movement (Gerwani) in 1966. Suharto maintained that women were a complement to men; the organisations introduced by the dictatorship were "housewife" organisations and family welfare groups.

There is still no mass women's movement that continuously campaigns for and organises women around women's issues. Many women's organisations are NGOs and research centres involved in various committees to support legal or parliamentary lobbying for reforms such as a 30% quota for women in legislatures or against domestic violence. These committees are usually institutionalised in the hands of several big NGOs and never develop into a mass movement. This partly explains why International Women's Day is still largely unknown.

Most oppressed

The poorest Indonesian women are workers, village housewives, young women and urban poor women. They suffer the most from the economic and political policies of the pro-imperialist government.

According to the Indonesian Health Demography Survey, in 2008 the maternal mortality rate was 320 per 100,000 births, the highest in Asia. Around 6.5 million Indonesian women are illiterate, twice the number of illiterate men, and women's participation in higher education is lower. According to the Indonesian Statistics Bureau, Jakarta region, women make up 88% of the unemployed in Jakarta.

These numbers are worsening because women are laid off more often than men because they are not considered family heads. When the economic crisis hit Indonesia in 1997, it largely destroyed manufacturing industries (garments, textiles, electronics and beverages). Female workers, who were mostly employed in those industries, were the ones who suffered massive lay-offs.

There are frequent violations of women's rights in the workplace. Workers' rights are still unknown by many female workers. They don't know that they have the right to unionise, to maternal leave and to menstruation leave with full payment. Female workers also receive lower wages than their male counterparts, especially in terms of allowances.

In this situation, poverty is an urgent problem for women. Capitalism and imperialism have destroyed women's chances of being economically independent. Cuts to education and health care subsidies and the privatisation of higher education have cost women the most. It's no wonder the Millennium Development Goals of lowering women's mortality and illiteracy rates have not been met. These facts are reinforced by the impact of the current capitalist economic crisis, which has made the prices of basic foods skyrocket.

There is no official prohibition on women enrolling in school but in a strongly patriarchal culture, women from poor families will always be second in line to receive education. The pro-imperialist government has nothing to lose from the fact that women are a minority in education, as it is also in favour of women being the cheapest reserve army of labour. It's not surprising that millions of Indonesian migrant workers, without proper skills and unfamiliar with workers' or women's rights, have been sent abroad, mostly as domestic workers. Many of them experience sexual abuse, rape, unwanted pregnancy, physical abuse and trauma, sometimes to the point of driving them to suicide.

Indonesian women are losing ground in regard to the democratic right to control their own bodies. There are now 151 regional sharia laws and "pornography laws" that regulate women's bodies and behaviour. It happens frequently that the sharia laws are used to criminalise female workers or prostitutes. They are also used as justification by some reactionary Islamic groups that frighten and abuse women - mostly prostitutes or women who have to work until late at night on the street.

The rights of women to fully control their own bodies, including having access to safe abortion, is still very far out of reach.

Perempuan Mahardhika

The organisation Perempuan Mahardhika (Free Women) was established in Jakarta in 2006 as a tool for female activists struggling for women's rights in different areas of society. Perempuan Mahardhika organises working women, female students, village or peasant women and urban poor women. It has been fully involved in the struggle for the liberation of the Indonesian people and of women through political activities, cultural struggles and grassroots organisation. Perempuan Mahardhika is aware that fundamental change can take place only if it involves the direct participation of women and all working people.

Perempuan Mahardhika believes that the struggle for the liberation and equality of women means a struggle to change society, the economic system and power. Unity in struggle and a mass women's movement are key methods to win the demands of the majority of women. That is why Perempuan Mahardhika always takes part in or initiates the support of any women's demand in the form of mass action and mobilisation. International Women's Day is one of the occasions on which Mahardhika has campaigned every year since 2006.

This year, Perempuan Mahardhika, together with different left and democratic forces, commemorated IWD in seven cities: Medan (North Sumatra), Jakarta, Yogyakarta, Makassar (South Sulawesi), Ternate (North Maluku), Samarinda (East Kalimantan) and Mojokerto (East Java). The general theme was SBY [President Susilo Bambang Yudhoyono] and [Vice-President] Boediono, parliamentary political parties and elites have failed to maintain democracy, to provide welfare and to protect women from exploitation, violence and sexual discrimination. There were also specific demands according to the situation in each city.

In Jakarta, Perempuan Mahardhika supported the Committee of Women's Liberation, which campaigns mostly for female workers rights like maternity and menstruation leave, against sexual harassment in the workplace, for reasonable wages and the protection of domestic workers and female migrant workers, employment that is productive and free from exploitation, free health care and education and against discrimination against LGBT people.

In Yogyakarta, Perempuan Mahardhika supported the Indonesian Women's Movement, which has similar demands with stress on the need to abolish or revise all discriminatory laws, such as the pornography law, anti-prostitution regional laws and the 1974 marriage law. In Makassar, Samarinda and Ternate, the demands were similar.

Ironically, in Yogyakarta most of the female NGOs in the committee named Yogyakarta Women's Network held an action calling on people to hug each other to commemorate IWD. They also shook hands and said "Happy Women's Day" to people in the street. Do they know how rare happy days are for the majority of women in Indonesia's economic and political system? History has shown there will be no achievement of women's rights without confronting patriarchal and capitalist governments and those confrontations are life and death struggles for most women.

[Zely Ariane is an activist with Perempuan Mahardhika and national spokesperson of the Political Committee of the Poor-Peoples Democratic Party (KPRM-PRD).]

Extracts statistics from UNITED NATIONS, 'Direct Action' Indonesia and direct quote from and according to the *Indonesian Statistics* Bureau, Jakarta region, *Women* are 88% of **...** Islamic groups that frighten and *abuse women* - mostly prostitutes or *women.*